Latin
THREE

FOR COMMON ENTRANCE

N. R. R. Oulton

About the author

Nicholas Oulton read History at Oriel College, Oxford and has an MA in Classics from London University. He taught Latin and Greek for ten years before writing the *So you really want to learn Latin* course and founding Galore Park in 1998.

Acknowledgements

The author and the publisher would like to thank Stephen Anderson for his generosity and support in producing this book. Stephen studied classics at Trinity College, Dublin and St John's College, Cambridge. From 1980 to 2015 he taught at Winchester College, where he was Head of Classics from 1984 to 2008 and subsequently Senior Tutor. In October 2015 he took up a new post as Lecturer in Classical Languages at New College, Oxford.

The publishers would like to thank the following for permission to reproduce copyright material:

Photo credits p9 © DEA / G. DAGLI ORTI/De Agostini/Getty Image **p50** © Eric James / Alamy Stock Photo **p65** © Ben Groves - Fotolia **p78** © Ashmolean Museum, University of Oxford, UK / Bridgeman Images **p89** © The Art Archive / Alamy Stock Photo

Every effort has been made to trace all copyright holders, but if any have been inadvertently overlooked, the publishers will be pleased to make the necessary arrangements at the first opportunity.

Although every effort has been made to ensure that website addresses are correct at time of going to press, Galore Park cannot be held responsible for the content of any website mentioned in this book. It is sometimes possible to find a relocated web page by typing in the address of the home page for a website in the URL window of your browser.

Hachette UK's policy is to use papers that are natural, renewable and recyclable products and made from wood grown in sustainable forests. The logging and manufacturing processes are expected to conform to the environmental regulations of the country of origin.

Orders: please contact Hachette UK Distribution, Hely Hutchinson Centre, Milton Road, Didcot, Oxfordshire, OX11 7HH. Telephone: +44 (0)1235 827827. Email education@hachette.co.uk. Lines are open from 9 a.m to 5 p.m, Monday to Friday. You can also 8order through our website: www.hoddereducation.com.

ISBN: 9781471867453

Text copyright © N.R.R. Oulton 2016

First published in 2016 by

Galore Park Publishing Ltd,

An Hachette UK Company

Carmelite House

50 Victoria Embankment

London EC4Y 0DZ

www.galorepark.co.uk

Impression number   10 9 8 7 6 5 4 3 2 1

Year   2020 2019 2018 2017 2016

Cover photo © ROMAOSLO - istockphoto.com

Artwork on page 39 by Aptara, Inc.

All other artworks by Integra Software Services, Ltd.

Typeset in India

Printed and bound by CPI Group (UK) Ltd, Croydon, CR0 4YY

A catalogue record for this title is available from the British Library.

Contents

Scholarship section

Introduction

In this third book in the course, we meet some of the more important Latin constructions and continue to follow some of the great stories of Roman history and Greek mythology. I am grateful to my hero, F. Ritchie, whose Latin exercises and passages for translation have helped generations of school pupils through the early stages of this great language since the 1880s. Particular use has been made of Ritchie's *Fabulae Faciles* when composing some of the passages drawn from Greek mythology, and I hope he will look down reasonably favourably on the results.

In terms of exam syllabuses, Level 3 of the ISEB CE exam is covered in the first seven chapters, and the material on the CASE syllabus is covered in the final three chapters. Those who make it through to the end will be well set to take those exams and to embark on the GCSE syllabus with a good grounding in the essential grammar and syntax.

Notes on features in this book

Exercise

Exercises are provided to give you plenty of opportunities to practise what you have learned.

> Useful rules and reminders are scattered throughout the book.

The box on the right makes it clear that you are studying a non-linguistic topic required by the ISEB Classics syllabus. Non-linguistic topics are about:

> This topic is part of the Non-Linguistic Studies section of the ISEB syllabus.

- aspects of domestic life in Rome
- early Roman legends
- Roman entertainment
- the Roman army
- Roman Britain
- Greek mythology.

Go further

This heading highlights material that is beyond the requirements of the ISEB syllabus. You do not need to remember this material for your exam, but it will help you understand some interesting aspects of the language.

1 Present passive; numerals 1–1000; place and time

The passive

So far, all the verbs you have met have been **active**. The subject of an active verb is the person or thing *doing the verb*.

E.g. The master *is teaching* the pupil.

But when the verb is **passive**, the subject of the verb is the person or thing to whom the verb is *being done*.

E.g. The pupil *is being taught* by the master.

Learning the passive tenses is relatively straightforward if you remember the following conversion chart for the verb endings:

	Active	Passive
1st person singular	-ō	-or
2nd person singular	-s	-ris
3rd person singular	-t	-tur
1st person plural	-mus	-mur
2nd person plural	-tis	-minī
3rd person plural	-nt	-ntur

Present passive

The present passive of amō, moneō, regō, audiō and capiō is shown below.

am-or	mone-or	reg-or	audi-or	capi-or
amā-ris	monē-ris	reg-eris	audī-ris	cap-eris
amā-tur	monē-tur	reg-itur	audī-tur	cap-itur
amā -mur	monē-mur	reg-imur	audī-mur	cap-imur
amā-minī	monē-minī	reg-iminī	audī-minī	cap-iminī
ama-ntur	mone-ntur	reg-untur	audi-untur	capi-untur

Note that capiō seems to have a certain amount of trouble determining whether its stem is cap- or capi-. As we saw in Book 1 when we first met capiō, the answer to this is that when two vowels come together (e.g. capiō, capiunt, capiam, etc.) the stem is capi- (and the verb is following the 4th conjugation). Where this does not happen (e.g. capis, capit, etc.), the stem is cap- (and it is following the 3rd conjugation).

Exercise 1.1

Study the information above about the passive. Then, for each of the following, write out the present tense, passive:

1 portō   2 teneō   3 iaciō   4 dūcō   5 inveniō

Exercise 1.2

Translate into English:

1 agricola vidētur.

2 puerī audiuntur.

3 dōnum datur.

4 mīles dūcitur.

5 servī interficiuntur.

6 mīlitēs ā duce iubentur.

7 iuvenēs ā rēge laudantur.

8 vōx puellae audītur.

9 oppidum nostrum dēfenditur.

10 urbs magna oppugnātur.

Exercise 1.3

Translate into Latin:

1 The city is ruled.

2 You (sing.) are warned.

3 They are being praised.

4 The slaves are being taught.

5 The temple is being destroyed.

6 The daughters of the mother are being watched.

7 All the soldiers are being killed.

8 The city is being defended in vain.

9 The women are found in the temple.

10 The book is given to your friend.

Go further

The historic present

It is very common in Latin to use a present tense when referring to the past. This technique, the **historic present**, is used in telling stories and is supposed to make the story more vivid by bringing the action into the present. When you see a present tense being used which clearly refers to the past, as in the passage below, it is good practice to translate it as a past tense.

Exercise 1.4

Translate into English:

Saved by the geese

Rōma ā Gallīs oppugnātur. mīlitēs Rōmānī in <u>summum</u> montem <u>ascendunt.</u> sed senēs, quod in <u>forō</u> manent, ā Gallīs inveniuntur. omnēs senēs interficiuntur et cīvēs Rōmānī terrentur. urbs tamen ab ānseribus sacrīs servātur. <u>anserēs</u> enim Gallōs audiunt et ululant. Gallī dē monte pelluntur et fugere cōguntur.

> summus, -a, -um = top
> ascendō, -ere = I go up
> forum, -ī, n. = the forum
> ānser, ānseris, m. = goose

Passive infinitives

The present infinitive of a verb may be made passive as shown below. Note how it is generally formed by changing the e of the active infinitive to an ī but, as always, regō and capiō are a little awkward.

amārī	monērī	regī	audīrī	capī
To be loved	To be warned	To be ruled	To be heard	To be captured

Exercise 1.5

Translate into English:

1 nūntiārī
2 redūcī
3 colligī
4 līberārī
5 pūnīrī
6 trādī
7 vulnerārī
8 vincī
9 movērī
10 iubērī

Translate into Latin:

1 To be related
2 To be greeted
3 To be handed over
4 To be conquered
5 To be saved
6 To be built
7 To be given
8 To be shown
9 To be sung
10 To be prepared

Numerals 1–1000

Now is a good time to revise the Roman numerals you have already met, those from 1 to 20 and 1st to 10th, and then add the cardinals from 21 to 100, and 1000. For Common Entrance you don't actually need to know the Latin for 500, but it is impossible to build large numbers (such as dates) without it, so we have included it in the table below.

Note that the numerals we use in English (1, 2, 3, etc.) are called Arabic numerals, to distinguish them from Roman numerals (I, II, III, etc.).

	Numerals	Cardinals	Ordinals
1	I	ūnus	prīmus
2	II	duŏ	secundus
3	III	trēs	tertius
4	IV	quattuor	quārtus
5	V	quīnque	quīntus
6	VI	sex	sextus
7	VII	septem	septimus
8	VIII	octo	octāvus
9	IX	novem	nōnus
10	X	decem	decimus
11	XI	ūndecim	
12	XII	duodecim	
13	XIII	tredecim	
14	XIV	quattuordecim	
15	XV	quīndecim	
16	XVI	sēdecim	
17	XVII	septendecim	
18	XVIII	duodēvīgintī	
19	XIX	ūndēvīgintī	
20	XX	vīgintī	
30	XXX	trīgintā	

	Numerals	Cardinals	Ordinals
40	XL	quadrāgintā	
50	L	quīnquāgintā	
60	LX	sexāgintā	
70	LXX	septuāgintā	
80	LXXX	octōgintā	
90	XC	nōnāgintā	
100	C	centum	
500	D	quīngentī	
1000	M	mīlle	

Go further

Building large numbers

As with numbers in English, large numbers in Latin were rarely written out in words, and so you need to know how to build up Roman numerals in blocks (thousands, hundreds, tens, units).

E.g.   35 = 30 + 5 = XXX + V = XXXV

879 = 800 + 70 + 9 = DCCC + LXX + IX = DCCCLXXIX

2225 = 2000 + 200 + 20 + 5 = MM + CC + XX + V = MMCCXXV

Notice how a smaller numeral placed before a larger one can be used to *reduce* the size of the larger one. Thus:

I can be used in front of V and X: e.g. IV = 4, IX = 9

X can be used in front of C and L: e.g. XL = 40, XC = 90

C can be used in front of M: e.g. CM = 900

Exercise 1.7

Study the information above about Roman numerals. Then translate into English:

1 novem puellae
2 duodēvīgintī equī
3 quadrāgintā senēs
4 quattuordecim servī
5 mīlle mīlitēs

6 nōnāgintā corpora
7 centum nāvēs
8 quīntus iuvenis
9 trīgintā tēla
10 septuāgintā virī

Exercise 1.8

Write in Roman numerals:

1	37	6	150
2	41	7	300
3	56	8	845
4	64	9	900
5	88	10	1050

Exercise 1.9

Write in Arabic numerals:

1	XLV	6	XLI
2	CCLIV	7	LXI
3	DCCLIII	8	LXXXIX
4	MLXVI	9	MML
5	LII	10	MCMXCIX

Exercise 1.10

From which Latin words do the following derive? Translate the Latin word and explain the meaning of the English one, showing the connection between the English and Latin. It may help to know that the Roman year began in March.

1	Octet	6	Quartet
2	Quintuplets	7	Secondary
3	Duet	8	Century
4	November	9	Millennium
5	Tertiary	10	December

Towns, small islands ...

Now for a wonderful rule about towns and small islands:

When going to or from *towns* and *small islands*, you must *not* use a preposition.

This rule applies to *the names of* towns (Rome, Troy, etc.) and *the names of* small islands (Ithaca, Rhodes, etc.). It does not apply to the word 'town' itself (i.e. oppidum), or to the words īnsula parva = 'small island'. It is only *named* towns or small islands.

Thus, if you are walking '*to* Rome', Rōmam ambulās. Rome goes in the accusative, as it would have done after the preposition ad, but the ad is not used. Similarly, if you are walking '*from* Rome', Rōmā ambulās, where Rome is in the ablative as it would have been after the preposition ā/ab.

Thus:

He walks to Rome from Troy = Rōmam Troiā ambulat.

He sails from Ithaca to Sicily = Ithacā ad Siciliam nāvigat.

(In this second example, Ithaca is classed as a small island, whereas Sicily is not.)

But (of course):

He walks to the town = ad oppidum ambulat.

He sails to the small island = ad īnsulam parvam nāvigat.

If, by the way, a preposition *is* used, it means 'to the neighbourhood of ...'.

E.g. ad Rōmam ambulō = I am walking to the neighbourhood of Rome.

Exercise 1.11

Read the rule about towns and small islands above. Then translate into English:

1 Londinium ambulābat.

2 Troiā discesserant.

3 Rōmam festīnābant.

4 Ithacam mox nāvigābimus.

5 nōnne ā Crētā nāvigāvistis?

6 ad oppidum magnum ambulāmus.

7 ad īnsulam parvam nāvigābat.

8 ad urbem ex oppidō festīnābam.

9 Rōmam Troiā festīnābat.

10 Troiam numquam nāvigāvērunt.

Read the following passage and answer the questions below.

The labours of Hercules: the Nemean lion

Herculēs, fīlius Alcmēnae et Iovis, omnium Graecōrum validissimus erat. Iunō, tamen, quod Alcmēnam ōderat, eī nocēre semper voluit. ōlim duās serpentēs in cubiculum eius dea mīsit, sed Herculēs, etiamtum īnfāns, eās occīdit. post multōs annōs, Iunō iuvenem iterum oppugnāvit et īn furōrem ēgit. propter furōrem,
5 Herculēs līberōs suōs occīdit. trīstissimus erat et ad ōrāculum īvit. hīc Pythia, fēmina sapientissima, iuvenem ita iussit: 'ad rēgem Eurystheum festīnā,' inquit, 'et prō eō duodecim labōrēs cōnfice.'

Eurystheus laetissimus erat. leō saevus illō tempore* in valle habitābat et rēx eum occīdere magnopere cupiēbat. 'ā leōne semper terrēmur,' rēx inquit. 'nunc ab
10 hōc perīculō līberāri possumus.'

Herculem igitur in vallem Nemeaeam mīsit. ille, sine mōrā, leōnem sagittīs oppugnāvit, nec tamen eum superāre poterat. pellis enim leōnis dēnsissima erat nec sagittae eam trāiēcērunt. tum magnā clāvā leōnem percussit, sed frūstrā.

tandem, iuvenis fortis collum leōnis manibus suīs compressit et feram superāvit.
15 corpus ad oppidum Eurystheī in umerīs portāvit et pellem leōnis posteā prō veste gerēbat.

* See below on expressions of time

Iuppiter, Iovis, m. = Jupiter	vallis, -is, f. = valley
ōdī = I hate (ōderam = I hated)	Nemeaeus, -a, -um = of Nemea
noceō, -ēre (+ dat.) = I harm	pellis, -is, f. = skin, hide
serpēns, -entis, f. = serpent	dēnsus, -a, -um = thick
cubiculum, -ī, n. = bedroom	trāiciō, -ere, trāiēcī = I pierce
etiamtum = (while) still	clāva, -ae, f. = club
infāns, infantis, c. = infant	percutiō, -ere, percussī = I strike
furor, furōris, m. = fury	collum, -ī, n. = neck
agō, agere, ēgī = I drive	manibus (abl.) = with his hands
ōrāculum, -ī, n. = oracle	comprimō, -ere, compressī = I squeeze
Pythia, -ae, f. = the Pythia (a priestess)	fera, -ae, f. = wild beast
cōnficiō, -ere = I complete	umerus, -ī, m. = shoulder
leō, leōnis, m. = lion	vestis, -is, f. = clothing
tempus, -oris, n. = time	

1 Herculēs ... erat (line 1). Who was Hercules and how is he described?

2 Iunō ... voluit (lines 1–2). Why did Juno want to harm Hercules?

3 ōlim ... occīdit (lines 2–3). How did Juno try to dispose of Hercules when he was still an infant?

4 post multōs annōs ... ēgit (lines 3–4). What did Juno do to him many years later?

5 propter furōrem ... occīdit (lines 4–5). What was the effect of Juno's actions?

6 trīstissimus ... cōnfice (lines 5–7). Explain what happened when Hercules visited the oracle.

7 laetissimus (line 8). What part of which adjective is this? Translate it.

8 mīsit (line 11). What part of which verb is this? Translate it.

9 illō tempore (line 8). Read the information below about expressions of time, and then explain the case of these words.

10 eum (line 12). What part of which pronoun is this? To whom or what does it refer?

11 From the second and third paragraphs (lines 8–13), give and translate:

  (a) a present infinitive active

  (b) an adverb

  (c) a present infinitive passive.

12 Translate the passage into English.

■ Hercules and the Nemean lion, depicted on a wine jug from Ancient Greece

◯ Expressions of time

Expressions of time in Latin are expressed according to the rules of the following rhyme:

Expressions of time you may learn by this rhyme,
Prepositions you never must use;
'Within which' and 'when': use the ablative case,
But for time 'how long': use the accus.

Use this rhyme to help you learn the following rules:

1 If you wish to describe *when* something happened, you use the ablative case.
   E.g. In the second year = secundō annō.
2 If you wish to describe a period of time *within which*, or *during which* something happened, again you must use the ablative case.
   E.g. Within five years = quīnque annīs.
   E.g. During the third hour = tertiā hōrā.
   N.B. in the expression 'by night' or 'during the night', noctū may be used instead of nocte.
3 If you wish to describe the duration of a period of time, i.e. say *how long* it lasted, you use the accusative case. Occasionally the preposition per is used.
   E.g. For two years = duōs annōs.

Note that it is not strictly true to say that you should *never* use prepositions with expressions of time. For example, in a phrase such as 'after six years', it would obviously be correct to use the preposition post + accusative.

Exercise 1.13

Study the information above about expressions of time. Then translate into Latin:

1 For five years

2 Within nine hours

3 During the night

4 During the third hour

5 In the fifth year

6 For eight nights

7 For seven hours

8 In the sixth year

9 After four nights

10 For many years

Exercise 1.14

Translate into English:

1 multōs annōs Rōmānī rēgēs timēbant.

2 prīmō annō Rōmulus urbem regēbat.

3 rēx saevus frātrem gladiō interfēcerat.

4 'multōs annōs' inquit 'Aenēās ad Ītaliam nāvigāvit.'

5 posteā cīvis fortis, nōmine Brūtus, rēgem ex urbe pepulit.

6 rēx Etruscōrum, nōmine Lars Porsenna, Rōmam festīnāvit.

7 Horātius urbem multās hōrās dēfendēbat nec tamen hostēs superāvit.

8 tandem Gallī urbem magnam noctū oppugnāvērunt.

9 mīlitēs Rōmānī dormiēbant sed mediā nocte iuvenēs clāmāvērunt.

10 multās hōrās Rōmānī cum hostibus pugnābant.

Go further

The locative case

We have seen above how we do not use prepositions when going to or from towns and small islands. The same applies when you are *in* a town or small island. With the names of towns and small islands, the **locative case** is used, without a preposition, to express location. The locative case ceased to exist as a separate form back in the early years of Latin's existence, so it had to be represented by one of the cases which *were* around. As a general rule, for singular place names of the 1st and 2nd declensions, the genitive was used; for 3rd declension and for all plural place names, the ablative was used.

Thus:

Rōma, -ae, f. = Rome	Locative: Rōmae = in Rome
Corinthus, -ī, f. = Corinth	Locative: Corinthī = in Corinth
Carthāgō, -inis, f. = Carthage	Locative: Carthāgine = in Carthage
Athēnae, -ārum, f. pl. = Athens	Locative: Athēnīs = in Athens

Vocabulary 1

Latin	English
Numerals	
trīgintā	thirty
quadrāgintā	forty
quīnquāgintā	fifty
sexāgintā	sixty
septuāgintā	seventy
octōgintā	eighty
nōnāgintā	ninety
centum	one hundred
mīlle	one thousand
Verbs	
cōgō, cōgere, coēgī, coāctum	I compel, force
interficiō, -ere, interfēcī, interfectum	I kill
pellō, -ere, pepulī, pulsum	I drive

Coming of age

The sons of Roman citizens marked their entry into adulthood at a coming-of-age ceremony when they were around 14 years of age. At the ceremony, the boy would approach the shrine of his family's household gods, the lārārium, and dedicate his toga praetexta (which he had worn since childhood), and his bulla (a sort of lucky charm worn around the neck), to the household gods (lārēs). He would then put on the plain white toga of an adult, the toga virilis. The boy was now considered to be an adult, and was eligible to vote in elections.

For girls, there was no such coming-of-age ceremony. A girl was considered to be an adult when she married, which she might do from the age of 12.

> This topic is part of the Non-Linguistic Studies section of the ISEB syllabus.

Marriage

For most Romans, marriage was arranged by their parents when they were still quite young. An engagement party (spōnsālia) was held to mark the contract between bride and groom, and the dowry to be given by the bride's father to the groom was agreed. At the ceremony itself, the bride wore a long white dress (tunica recta), and her hair was decorated with flowers and a bright orange veil. The marriage contract was signed and the bride and groom joined hands. After the ceremony there was a feast

> This topic is part of the Non-Linguistic Studies section of the ISEB syllabus.

(cēna nuptiālis), and at the end of this it was customary for the bride to pretend not to wish to leave her parents, and the groom ceremoniously snatched her away and carried her off to his house. When they reached his house, the groom would ask his new wife who she was, to which she would give the traditional reply 'ubi tū Gaius, ego Gaia' (i.e. 'Where you are Gaius, I am Gaia'). This symbolised her submission to her husband, but also the fact that they were now a family.

Exercise 1.15

Find out what you can about Roman coming-of-age and marriage ceremonies, and about Hercules and his twelve labours. Then answer the questions below.

(a) (i)   You live in ancient Rome and have just returned from attending your sister's wedding. Describe the events of the day.

   (ii)   How might the day have differed from a typical wedding in modern-day Britain?

(b) (i)   Write an account of your ancient Roman older brother's coming-of-age ceremony.

   (ii)   Which features of the day might appear strange to someone living in modern-day Britain?

(c) (i)   How did Hercules overcome the Nemean lion?

   (ii)   Explain briefly why Hercules found himself tasked with completing his twelve labours.

Future and imperfect passive; agents and instruments; 5th declension

Future passive

The future passive tells us what *will be done* to the subject, e.g. I will be loved. Note how the -bō, -bis, -bit endings become -bor, -beris, -bitur, whereas the -am, -ēs, -et endings become -ar, -ēris, -ētur.

amā-bor	monē-bor	reg-ar	audi-ar	capi-ar
amā-beris	monē-beris	reg-ēris*	audi-ēris	capi-ēris
amā-bitur	monē-bitur	reg-ētur	audi-ētur	capi-ētur
amā-bimur	monē-bimur	reg-ēmur	audi-ēmur	capi-ēmur
amā-biminī	monē-biminī	reg-ēminī	audi-ēminī	capi-ēminī
amā-buntur	monē-buntur	reg-entur	audi-entur	capi-entur

* This looks almost identical to the 2nd person singular, present passive (regeris); only the pronunciation is different.

Exercise 2.1

Write out the future passive of the following verbs:

1 superō, superāre

2 pōnō, pōnere

3 videō, vidēre

4 iaciō, iacere

5 inveniō, invenīre

Exercise 2.2

Translate into English:

1 omnēs cīvēs ex urbe fugere cōgentur.

2 post proelium iuvenēs et senēs ā rēge saevō interficientur.

3 equī ex agrīs ab agricolā pellentur.

4 Rōmānī ab hostibus numquam superābuntur.

5 puer miser ā rēgīnā vidērī nōn volēbat.

6 templum magnum ā servīs fessīs aedificārī nōn poterat.

7 num vīnum optimum sorōrī meae trādētur?

8 nōnne nāvis tempestāte paucīs hōrīs dēlēbitur?

9 mīles fortis ā custōdibus crūdēlibus multōs annōs pūniētur.

10 num illī quīndecim senēs ab hīs quattuor mīlitibus custōdientur?

Imperfect passive

The imperfect passive tells us what *was being done* to the subject, e.g. I was being loved. Notice how -bam, -bās, -bat becomes -bar, -bāris, -bātur, etc.

amā-bar	monē-bar	reg-ēbar	audi-ēbar	capi-ēbar
amā-bāris	monē-bāris	reg-ēbāris	audi-ēbāris	capi-ēbāris
amā-bātur	monē-bātur	reg-ēbātur	audi-ēbātur	capi-ēbātur
amā-bāmur	monē-bāmur	reg-ēbāmur	audi-ēbāmur	capi-ēbāmur
amā-bāminī	monē-bāminī	reg-ēbāminī	audi-ēbāminī	capi-ēbāminī
amā-bantur	monē-bantur	reg-ēbantur	audi-ēbantur	capi-ēbantur

Exercise 2.3

Write out the imperfect passive of the following verbs:

1 oppugnō, oppugnāre

2 scrībō, scrībere

3 moveō, movēre

4 accipiō, accipere

5 pūniō, pūnīre

Translate the following passage.

Hercules and the Lernaean Hydra

Eurystheus, post mortem <u>leōnis</u> <u>Nemeaeī</u>, Herculem <u>serpentem</u> maximam interficere iussit. haec <u>serpēns</u>, nōmine Hydra, novem capita habēbat et in <u>palūde</u> <u>Lernaeā</u> habitābat. Herculēs, cum amīcō Iolāō, ad <u>palūdem</u> adiit: serpentem invēnit, corpus eius <u>sinistrā</u> cēpit, <u>dextrā</u> capita <u>abscīdere</u> <u>coepit</u>.

5　　<u>quotiēns</u> tamen caput <u>abscīderat</u>, novum caput <u>appārēbat</u>. opus, quod Herculēs ā <u>cancrō</u> saevō <u>mordēbātur</u>, difficillimum erat, sed tandem ille <u>serpentem</u> superāvit. <u>colla</u> enim <u>face</u> <u>adūssit</u> nec capita <u>crēscere</u> poterant. postquam Hydram interfēcit, Herculēs sagittās suās <u>sanguine</u> <u>mortiferō</u> eius <u>imbuit</u>. tum ad Eurystheum rediit.

leō, leōnis, m. = lion	appāreō, -ēre = I appear
Nemeaeus, -a, -um = of Nemea	cancer, cancrī, m. = crab
serpēns, serpentis, f. = serpent	mordeō, -ēre = I bite
palūs, -ūdis, f. = marsh	collum, -ī, n. = neck
Lernaeus, -a, -um = of Lerna	fax, facis, f. = fire-brand, torch
sinistra, -ae, f. = left hand	adūrō, -ere, adūssī = I scorch
dextra, -ae, f. = right hand	crēscō, -ere = I grow
abscīdō, -ere = I cut off	sanguis, -inis, m. = blood
coepī = I begin	mortiferus, -a, -um = deadly
quotiēns = as often as, whenever	imbuō, -ere = I soak

Agents and instruments

The passive is often followed by an ablative to tell us by whom or what the action of the verb is being done. If this is *a person or animal*, it is an **agent** and must have the preposition ā/ab. If it is a *thing*, it is an **instrument** and has no preposition.

E.g. He is loved by the *girl* (agent) = ā puellā amātur.

E.g. He is killed with a *sword* (instrument) = gladiō interficitur.

Study the information above about agents and instruments. Then translate into Latin:

1　They will be punished by the cruel king.

2　He made a long journey with the soldiers.

3 Many messengers will be sent by the queen.

4 The fortunate slaves will not be killed by the sword.

5 The soldiers are being sent to Rome by the leader.

6 She was being warned by the master.

7 They will be thrown into the river by the farmer.

8 The city of the enemy was being attacked with arrows.

9 Beautiful words were being written by the poet.

10 The children of the master will be terrified by the storm.

5th declension nouns: rēs

There are five declensions in Latin, but we are going to skip the 4th, and move straight on to the 5th. Nouns of the 5th declension decline like rēs. They are all feminine except diēs = 'day' and merīdiēs = 'noon', which are masculine (actually even diēs is feminine when it refers to an *appointed* day).

N.B. Nouns in -iēs (e.g. diēs) have a long -ē in the genitive and dative singular (e.g. diēī).

rēs, reī, f. = thing, affair		
	Singular	Plural
Nominative	rēs	rēs
Vocative	rēs	rēs
Accusative	rem	rēs
Genitive	reī	rērum
Dative	reī	rēbus
Ablative	rē	rēbus

Exercise 2.6

Study the information above about 5th declension nouns. Write out the following:

1 diēs, diēī, m. = day – singular and plural

2 fidēs, fideī, f. = faith, trust – singular only

3 spēs, speī, f. = hope – singular only

Exercise 2.7

Translate into Latin:

1 That man remained in the city for five days.

2 They will attack Rome within seven days.

3 The leader had great hope on account of his faith.

4 We are always driven by our hope.

5 The affairs of the city were being praised by the citizens.

Exercise 2.8

Translate into English:

Manlius Torquatus, 361 BC

ōlim Gallī Rōmam oppugnāre cupiēbant. mīlitēs eōrum ā prīncipe fortī dūcēbantur nec tamen urbs capiēbātur. inter mīlitēs Rōmānōs erat Titus Mānlius. ille mīles fortissimus ab omnibus laudābātur. post multōs diēs Gallī Rōmānōs nōn superāverant et fessī erant. itaque Gallus <u>quīdam</u> ad Romānōs appropinquāvit.

5 corpus ingēns, <u>bracchia</u> ingentia habēbat et magnā vōce haec dīxit: 'nōnne ūnus Rōmānus' inquit 'cum ūnō Gallō pugnābit?' Rōmānī diū Gallum ingentem spectābant. <u>tandem</u> Titus Mānlius 'ego' inquit 'cum eō Gallō pugnābō.'

in <u>pugnā</u> Titus Mānlius Gallum ingentem interfēcit et <u>torquem</u> eius cēpit. ille, quod fidem in dīs posuerat, ā Rōmānīs laudābātur et propter <u>torquem</u>
10 Torquātus <u>appellābātur</u>.

> quīdam = a certain
> bracchium, -ī, n. = arm
> pugna, -ae, f. = fight
> torquis, -is, m. = necklace
> appellō, -āre = I name, call

Exercise 2.9

Study the words in Vocabulary 2, below. From which Latin words are the following derived? Translate the Latin word and explain the meaning of the English one.

1 Annual

2 Custodian

3 Tempestuous

4 Persuasive

5 Petition

Vocabulary 2

Latin	English
Nouns	
annus, -ī, m.	year
custōs, custōdis, m.	guard
diēs, diēī, m.	day (fem. if an appointed day)
fidēs, fideī, f.	trust, faith, promise
hōra, -ae, f.	hour
rēs, reī, f.	thing, affair
spēs, speī, f.	hope
tempestās, -ātis, f.	storm, weather
Verbs	
custōdiō, -īre, -īvī, -ītum	I guard
persuādeō, -ēre, persuāsī, persuāsum (+ dat.)	I persuade
petō, -ere, petīvī, petītum	I seek, make for

I Claudius …

We have already seen how Julius Caesar came to Britain in 44 and 43 BC, with only moderate success. Around a hundred years later, another famous Roman made the voyage across the English Channel in search of glory and a much needed military victory, to boost popularity back in Rome. This was the stammering and physically handicapped Emperor Claudius, who was determined to demonstrate to the people of Rome that he had the military prowess required to be emperor. In AD 43, Claudius sent four legions under Aulus Plautius across the Channel and this mighty force had soon defeated the British tribesmen led by Caratacus and driven them back to Camulodunum (Colchester). Claudius himself then crossed, together with a herd of war elephants, to witness the fall of Colchester. Sixteen days later, Claudius returned to Rome to celebrate his success in a military triumph, leaving his generals to continue the conquest of the country without him.

> This topic is part of the Non-Linguistic Studies section of the ISEB syllabus.

Find out what you can about Claudius's invasion of Britain in AD 43, and the subsequent campaigns of Aulus Plautius and Vespasian. You may find *Greeks & Romans* by A. M. Wright helpful. Then answer the following questions.

(a) (i) Give a brief account of Claudius's invasion of Britain and initial conquest of the country.

(ii) Do you think Claudius deserved to celebrate a military triumph as a result of his involvement in the campaign?

(b) (i) Draw a sketch-map of Britain, showing the route taken by Claudius's army in AD 43. Mark on the map the main towns and roads of Roman Britain.

(ii) Give two ways in which the Roman army would have proved superior to the British tribesmen they faced in battle.

(c) (i) How did Hercules overcome the Lernaean Hydra?

(ii) Why do you think he steeped his arrows in the Hydra's blood?

2 Future and imperfect passive; agents and instruments; 5th declension

3 The perfect and pluperfect passive; three termination adjectives

Perfect passive

The perfect passive tells us what *has been done* to the subject, e.g. 'I have been loved' or 'I was loved'. It is formed by taking the Perfect (or Past) Participle Passive (the PPP), and combining it with the verb 'to be'. The PPP of a verb is formed from the **supine stem**, found in the 4th principal part. All you have to do is change the -um to -us. (Now you know why we have been encouraging you to learn all four principal parts of your verbs.)

amāt-us, -a, -um	sum	I have been loved
amāt-us -a, -um	es	You (sing.) have been loved
amāt-us, -a, -um	est	He, she, it has been loved
amāt-ī, -ae, -a	sumus	We have been loved
amāt-ī, -ae, -a	estis	You (pl.) have been loved
amāt-ī, -ae, -a	sunt	They have been loved

Note that the PPP is an adjective, declining like bonus. If the subject is masculine and singular, the ending is -us. But if it is feminine, this becomes -a, and so on.

Thus: He has been loved (or was loved) = amātus est.
She has been loved (or was loved) = amāta est.
The boys have been loved (or were loved) = puerī amātī sunt.
The girls have been loved (or were loved) = puellae amātae sunt.

Exercise 3.1

Study the information above about the perfect passive. Write out the perfect passive (assuming a masculine subject) of:

1 moneō   2 regō   3 audiō   4 capiō

Exercise 3.2

Translate into English. Note how the PPP changes to agree with the subject. E.g. in sentence 1, missus becomes missae to agree with the subject (nāvēs, which is feminine plural).

1 paucae nāvēs ad īnsulam multīs cum mīlitibus* missae sunt.

2 mīles ā prīncipe novō laudātus est.

3 paucās noctēs urbs ab hostibus oppugnābātur.

4 puella per viās urbis ducta est.

5 hōra proeliī populō Rōmānō nūntiāta est.

6 'nostrī'** inquit 'ab hostibus numquam superābuntur.'

7 nunc cibus in oppidum ā līberīs prīncipis portātur.

8 ancillae miserae ā rēgīnā crūdēlī multōs diēs pūnītae sunt.

9 'auxilium' inquiunt 'ā cōpiīs novīs datum est.'

10 multī clāmōrēs in oppidō audītī sunt.

* multīs cum mīlitibus is more stylish Latin than cum multīs mīlitibus. The preposition likes to precede the noun, not the adjective. Therefore, as multus comes before its noun, rather than after it, the preposition has to dive in between it and the soldiers.

** Remember, when an adjective is used without a noun, you understand men in the masculine, women in the feminine and things in the neuter.

E.g. bonī semper laudantur = good men are always praised.

Exercise 3.3

Translate into Latin, remembering to make the PPP agree with the subject:

1 The boy has been called.

2 The girl has been called.

3 The war has been prepared.

4 The boys have been taught.

5 The girls have been watched.

6 The wars were waged by our men.

7 The soldiers have been seen by the enemy.

8 The city was attacked by a few slaves.

9 The Romans were terrified by the new king.

10 Part of the city was destroyed by the young men.

◯ Pluperfect passive

The pluperfect passive tells us what *had been done* to the subject.
This time it is the imperfect of sum that we add.

amāt-us, -a, -um	eram	I had been loved
amāt-us, -a, -um	erās	You (sing.) had been loved
amāt-us, -a, -um	erat	He, she, it had been loved
amāt-ī, -ae, -a	erāmus	We had been loved
amāt-ī, -ae, -a	erātis	You (pl.) had been loved
amāt-ī, -ae, -a	erant	They had been loved

Exercise 3.4

Read the information above about the pluperfect passive. Then translate into Latin:

1 She had been warned.

2 You (sing.) had been terrified.

3 The gift had been given to the small boy.

4 The enemy had been defeated by the Romans.

5 The leaders had been chosen already.

6 I had been forced to work for seven years.

7 She had been killed on the fifth day.

8 'Citizens, why had you not been warned?'

9 The king had been driven out of the city during the night.

10 The temple had been destroyed by the soldiers.

Exercise 3.5

Translate into English:

1 puerī puellaeque ā magistrō territī erant.

2 omnēs servī in agrōs pulsī erant.

3 puella misera in monte quīnque diēs manēre coācta erat.

4 nōnne senēs ē patriā mox pellentur?

5 fīlius prīncipis sub mūrō vīsus erat.

6 nāvis tempestāte magnā dēlēta erat.

7 custōdēs ā servīs in flūmen pulsī erant.

8 uxor rēgis ab ancillā interfecta erat.

9 tēla mīlitibus nautīsque data erant.

10 fīlia prīncipis multōs diēs petīta erat, sed frūstrā.

Read the following passage and answer the questions below.

The labours of Hercules: the cleaning of the Augean stables

postquam Herculēs <u>Hydram</u> occīdit, <u>cervum</u> <u>quendam</u> capere iussus est. per
tōtum annum iuvenis fortis et <u>cervus</u> celer currēbant sed tandem Herculēs
animal cēpit. inde <u>aprum</u> <u>Erymanthium</u> ad rēgem Eurystheum, <u>ut</u> iussus erat,
vīvum portāvit. post haec Eurystheus in <u>rēgnum</u> <u>Ēlidem</u> Herculem mīsit. hīc rēx
5   Augēas <u>tria mīlia boum</u>* habēbat. hī in <u>stabulō</u> ingentī <u>inclūsī</u> erant nec tamen
illud <u>stabulum</u> multōs annōs <u>pūrgātum</u> erat. Herculēs stabulum ūnō diē pūrgāre
iussus est. <u>hōc modō</u> ille labor <u>cōnfectus</u> est: prīmum, <u>fossam</u> Herculēs <u>fōdit</u> et
aquam flūminis de montibus ad mūrum <u>stabulī</u> dūxit. inde mūrum <u>frēgit</u> et aqua
in <u>stabulum fluxit</u>. <u>fimus</u> in flūmen <u>transportātus</u> est et omnis <u>stabulī</u> <u>illuviēs</u>
10   <u>pūrgāta</u> est.

*See Declining numerals, below.

Hydra, -ae, f. = the Hydra	pūrgō, -āre = I clean
cervus, -ī, m. = stag	hōc modō = in this way
quendam (acc.) = a certain	cōnficiō, -ere, cōnfēcī, cōnfectum = I
aper, aprī, m. = wild-boar	complete
Erymanthius, -a, -um = Erymanthian	fossa, -ae, f. = ditch
ut = as	fodiō, -ere, fōdī = I dig
rēgnum, -ī, n. = kingdom	frangō, -ere, frēgī, frāctum = I break
Ēlis, -idis, f. = Elis	fluō, -ere, fluxī, fluxum = I flow
tria mīlia boum = three thousand oxen	fimus, -ī, m. = dung
stabulum, -ī, n. = stable	transportō, -āre = I remove
inclūdō, -ere, inclūsī, inclūsum = I shut in	illuviēs, -ēī, f. = filth

1   Translate the passage into English.

2   occīdit (line 1). In which tense is this verb? Give its 1st person
singular of the present tense, active.

3   iussus est (line 1). Give the 1st person singular of the present
tense, active, of this verb.

4   currēbant (line 2). Put this verb into the future tense, keeping the
person and number the same.

5   iussus erat (line 3). In which tense is this verb?

6   haec (line 4). Give the nominative singular masculine and meaning
of this word.

7   hī (line 5).

    (a) In which case is this word?

    (b) Give its nominative singular masculine and meaning.

8 ingentī (line 5). In which case, number and gender is this word?

9 illud (line 6). In which case, number and gender is this word?

10 ūnō diē (line 6). In which case are these words, and why?

11 montibus (line 8).

   (a) In which case is this word?

   (b) Give its nominative singular masculine and meaning.

12 omnīs (line 9). In which case, number and gender is this word? With which word does it agree?

Go further

Declining numerals

You have met the numerals 1–1000, but there are one or two things to notice about these. First, the numbers 1–3 decline:

	Masc.	Fem.	Neut.
Nom.	ūnus	ūna	ūnum
Acc.	ūnum	ūnam	ūnum
Gen.	ūnius	ūnius	ūnius
Dat.	ūnī	ūnī	ūnī
Abl.	ūnō	ūnā	ūnō
Nom.	duŏ	duae	duŏ
Acc.	duōs/duŏ	duās	duŏ
Gen.	duōrum	duārum	duōrum
Dat.	duōbus	duābus	duōbus
Abl.	duōbus	duābus	duōbus
Nom.	trēs	trēs	tria
Acc.	trēs	trēs	tria
Gen.	trium	trium	trium
Dat.	tribus	tribus	tribus
Abl.	tribus	tribus	tribus

Second, the number mīlle = 1000 is an indeclinable adjective. However, if we wish to refer to more than one thousand, we use the 3rd declension neuter plural noun, mīlia, followed by the genitive. Thus two thousand soldiers = duo mīlia mīlitum.

This additional information about numerals explains the phrase in the passage above, tria mīlia boum = three thousand oxen.

Translate into English:

Filial disobedience, 340 BC

Mānlius Torquātus cōnsul erat cum Pūbliō Deciō. bellum eō annō cum Latīnīs Rōmānī gerēbant. ōlim Mānlius mīlitēs vocāvit et 'cum hostibus' inquit 'pugnāre nōn cupiō.' sed eques Latīnus magnā vōce 'Rōmānī' inquit 'pugnāre nōn cupiunt; Rōmānī Latīnōs timent.' fīlius autem Mānliī Torquātī verba eius audīvit. gladium
5 igitur cēpit et in hostēs cucurrit. eques Latīnus ā Rōmānō fortī vulnerātus et interfectus est.

pater, tamen, īrātus erat. 'nōnne' inquit 'verba mea audīvistī? cūr cum hostibus pugnāvistī?' tum fīlius miser ā patre captus est et gladiō interfectus est.

> cōnsul, cōnsulis, m. = consul
> eques, equitis, m. = horseman
> Latīnus, -a, -um = Latin (the Latins were a tribe near Rome)

Three termination adjectives

A small number of 3rd declension adjectives are said to be **three termination**, because in the nominative singular they have *three* different endings. E.g. ācer, ācris, ācre = keen, or celer, celeris, celere = swift. They decline exactly like trīstis, except for the fact that they have different masculine and feminine endings in the nominative and vocative singular.

	M	F	N
Nom.	celer	celeris	celere
Voc.	celer	celeris	celere
Acc.	celerem	celerem	celere
Gen.	celeris	celeris	celeris
Dat.	celerī	celerī	celerī
Abl.	celerī	celerī	celerī
Nom.	celerēs	celerēs	celeria
Voc.	celerēs	celerēs	celeria
Acc.	celerēs	celerēs	celeria
Gen.	celerium	celerium	celerium
Dat.	celeribus	celeribus	celeribus
Abl.	celeribus	celeribus	celeribus

Adjectives like this would originally have ended in -is in the nominative masculine singular, but at some stage in the dim and distant past the word seems to have changed. Notice also that some of these adjectives (e.g. ācer) drop their e, while others (e.g. celer) do not.

Exercise 3.8

Translate into English:

1 equī celerēs ab agricolā tandem captī sunt.

2 iuvenēs crūdēlēs ā magistrō pūnītī erant.

3 virī nōbilēs ab hostibus captī et interfectī sunt.

4 omnia opera poētae ā fēminīs laudāta erant.

5 comitēs ducis, quod timēbant, iuvenēs celerēs effugere volēbant.

6 custōdēs ab omnibus cīvibus diū petītī sunt.

7 uxor pulchra multōs annōs ā rēge amābātur.

8 agricolae animal celere capere nōn poterant.

9 prīnceps labōrēs iuvenis nōn laudābat.

10 nāvis prīncipis in īnsula parva relicta erat.

dum = while

The conjunction dum = while is usually followed by a verb in the present tense, which should be translated as if it were in the imperfect. This applies if dum is referring to a period of time during the course of which something else happened.

E.g. dum ambulat, puer equum vīdit = While the boy was walking he saw a horse.

If, however, dum is referring to a period of time which is coterminous with the thing that happened (i.e. both things were happening at the same time), then an imperfect tense is used in Latin.

E.g. dum ambulābāmus, cantābāmus = While we were walking, we were singing.

autem = moreover, however, now, and

While we are looking at conjunctions, it is important to note that autem, which we have met with the meaning however or moreover, is often used simply to introduce a new thought, and sometimes means little more than 'and' or 'now'. Study this exciting extract from a children's story:

Three little pigs lived in a house in the middle of a wood. *Now*, in that wood there was a wicked wolf ...

If we were putting this into Latin, the word *now* could best be translated with the Latin word autem.

Translate the following passage into English and then answer the questions below.

The Caudine Forks, 321 BC

dum cōpiae Rōmānae Ītaliam superant, tria bella cum Samnītibus gessērunt.
bellō autem secundō dux Samnītium, nōmine Gāius Pontius, castra prope
Caudium posuit. tum cōnsilium ita cēpit. decem peditēs in agrīs ambulāre iussit.
peditēs ā Rōmānīs captī sunt. 'mīlitēs Samnītium' inquiunt peditēs 'ad urbem
5　Lūceriam iam discessērunt.' Rōmānī Lūceriam festīnāvērunt quod urbem servāre
cupiēbant.
　　duae viae ad urbem ferēbant. erat prope mare via longa, per montēs via
brevis. Rōmānī per montēs iter faciēbant et in locō angustō, nōmine Furculīs
Caudīnīs, ā Samnītibus superātī sunt. Rōmānī ā Samnītibus pācem petere coāctī
10　sunt et omnēs mīlitēs sub iugum missī sunt.*

*To send an enemy under the yoke (sub iugum mittere) was a traditional form of humiliation.

Samnītēs, -ium, m. pl. = the Samnites (a tribe in Italy)	ferō = I lead (of a road)
	brevis, -e = short
castra, -ōrum, n. pl. = camp	angustus, -a, -um = narrow
cōnsilium, -ī, n. = plan	furcula, -ae, f. = fork
cōnsilium capiō = I adopt a plan	pāx, pācis, f. = peace
pedes, -itis, m. = foot-soldier	iugum, -ī, n. = yoke

1　superant (line 1). Explain the tense of this verb.

2　gessērunt (line 1). Give the principal parts of this verb.

3　posuit (line 3). What would this verb become if it were in the passive, with castra as its subject, keeping the tense the same?

4　ambulāre (line 3). What part of which verb is this?

5　captī sunt (line 4). In which tense is this verb? Give the Latin subject of the verb.

6　discessērunt (line 5). What part of which verb is this?

7　mare (line 7). In which case is this noun? Why is it in this case?

8　iter (line 8). In which case is this noun? Why is it in this case?

9　pācem (line 9). Explain the connection between this word and the English word **pacify**.

10　missī sunt (line 10). What part of which verb is this? Give its past participle passive (PPP).

◯ Vocabulary 3

Latin	English
Nouns	
animal, animālis, n.	animal
labor, labōris, m.	work, task, labour
nox, noctis, f.	night
opus, operis, n.	work
prīnceps, prīncipis, c.	chief, leader
Adjective	
celer, celeris, celere	swift, quick
Verbs	
petō, -ere, petīvī, petītum	I seek, make for
relinquō, -ere, relīquī, relictum	I leave
Conjunctions	
dum	while
nec	and not, nor
neque	and not, nor

◯ Towns in Roman Britain

We saw in the last chapter how the Romans came to conquer Britain following the invasion of Claudius in AD 43. During this period towns grew up, sometimes based on existing British settlements, but often new ones, based on Roman army camps. It was important that the town had a good water supply, and effective lines of communication such as roads or a navigable river. Towns were often built on a grid system, similar to the camps on which many of them were based, with the forum in the middle. They would usually have temples, a theatre, an amphitheatre, baths and of course, shops. Water might be brought into the town by an aqueduct, as at Lindum (Lincoln), which often fed not just the drinking water supply but also the baths. The names of many towns in Britain today end in -chester, which shows that they were once based on or near a Roman camp (castra).

> This topic is part of the Non-Linguistic Studies section of the ISEB syllabus.

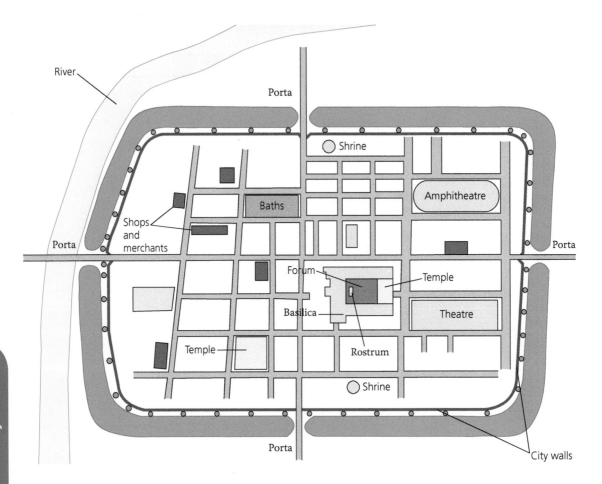

■ Diagram showing the buildings and the layout of a typical Roman town

Exercise 3.10

(a) (i) Tell the story of Manlius Torquatus and his son.

  (ii) How do you think the father would have behaved had this story happened today?

(b) (i) Draw a plan of a typical Roman town.

  (ii) Give two ways in which a Roman town would have been similar to a modern town in Britain today.

(c) (i) How did Hercules clean the Augean stables?

  (ii) In what ways did this labour demonstrate Hercules's cunning, as well as his strength?

 **Relative clauses**

A relative clause begins with a word such as 'who' or 'which' (a relative pronoun) and tells us more about the noun or pronoun to which it refers.

E.g. The girl, *who was walking to school,* ...

E.g. The hay-stack, *which we saw in the fields,* ...

In these examples the words in italics are relative clauses, telling us more about the nouns (the girl and the hay-stack) to which they refer.

The relative pronoun in Latin is quī, quae, quod:

quī, quae, quod = who, which:			
	M	**F**	**N**
Nom.	quī	quae	quod
Acc.	quem	quam	quod
Gen.	cuius	cuius	cuius
Dat.	cui*	cui*	cui*
Abl.	quō	quā	quō
Nom.	quī	quae	quae
Acc.	quōs	quās	quae
Gen.	quōrum	quārum	quōrum
Dat.	quibus**	quibus**	quibus**
Abl.	quibus**	quibus**	quibus**

* cui is a diphthong, pronounced as one syllable.

** Or quīs.

Antecedents

The noun to which a relative clause refers is called the **antecedent.** In Latin, the relative pronoun must agree with the antecedent in *gender* and *number.* Its *case* is determined by its grammatical relationship within the relative clause and will often be different from the case of the antecedent:

Antecedent	Relative clause	
The woman (nom.),	who (nom.) is walking ...	fēmina **quae** ambulat
The woman (nom.),	whom (acc.) we hear ...	fēmina **quam** audīmus
The woman (nom.),	whose (gen.) daughter we like ...	fēmina **cuius** fīliam amāmus
The woman (nom.),	to whom (dat.) we gave a present ...	fēmina **cui** dōnum dedimus
The woman (nom.),	by whom (abl.) he was killed ...	fēmina **ā quā** interfectus est

Exercise 4.1

Read the information above about relative clauses. Identify the antecedent, relative pronoun and relative clause in the following sentences. Then translate:

1 dominus, quī est in templō, īrātus est.

2 puella, quae est in agrō, cantat.

3 bellum, quod longum erat, fēminās terrēbat.

4 dominus, quem amāmus, miser est.

5 puella, quam in agrō vidēmus, cantat.

6 bellum, quod Rōmānī gerēbant, incolās terrēbat.

7 dominus, cuius servus fessus est, semper īrātus est.

8 puella, cuius māter dormit, semper cantat.

9 dux, cuius mīlitēs omnēs timēmus, ad oppidum iter faciēbat.

10 iam dominus, cui dōnum dedistī, laetus est.

Exercise 4.2

Translate into Latin:

1 The boy, who is singing ...

2 The girl, who is walking ...

3 The war, which we are waging ...

4 The boy, whom we see ...

5 The women, to whom we give ...

6 The farmers, who are working ...

7 With the soldier, whose ...

8 Of the young men, by whom ...

9 The river, in which ...

10 The enemy, who are fighting ...

Exercise 4.3

Identify the antecedent, relative pronoun and relative clause in the following sentences. Then translate into Latin:

1 The master, who was writing in the book, was very happy.

2 The girl, who was preparing the food, was very angry.

3 The soldier, whom we saw, was fighting.

4 The woman, whom we had warned, suddenly departed.

5 The leader, whose soldiers were fighting, was very bold.

6 The goddess, to whom we were singing, was very wise.

7 The inhabitants, by whom we were being watched, lived in the mountains.

8 The horses, which were in the field, were drinking water.

9 The rivers, which we saw, were very deep.

10 The soldiers, whom the leader had led into the town, were tired.

◯ Translating relative clauses

Sentences which contain relative clauses can cause problems if you are not careful. The key to success lies in knowing when to translate the relative clause. It is really very simple. You almost always translate the relative clause immediately *after you have translated the antecedent*. If the antecedent is not in the nominative case, this will involve waiting until you have got to it. Just be patient!

E.g.   dominum, quī est in templō, vidēmus =

We see the master, *who is in the temple.*

E.g.   māter puerī, quī est in templō, cantābat =

The mother of the boy, *who is in the temple,* was singing.

E.g.   dōnum amīcō meō, quī est in Graeciā, mīsī =

I have sent a gift to my friend, *who is in Greece.*

Beware when translating the word quod. This can sometimes be the neuter relative pronoun, sometimes the conjunction meaning 'because'.

Exercise 4.4

Study the information above about translating relative clauses. Then translate into English:

1 Pyrrhus, quī oppidum adībat, rēx magnus erat.

2 Rōmānī, quōs timēbāmus, incolīs crēdiderant.

3 librōs, quōs mihi dedistī, lentē legam.

4 rēx, cuius mīlitēs spectābāmus, fortissimus est.

5 bellum contrā Rōmānōs, quī urbem oppugnāverant, gessimus.

6 intereā sociōs per viās urbis, quam oppugnāverās, dūcēbās.

7 quod omnēs magnopere timēbant, propter perīcula ex urbe contendimus.

8 tēlum in flūmine, quod prope urbem est, invēnit.

9 soror ducis ad urbem rediit et cīvēs monuit.

10 cīvēs optimī, quī urbem amant, semper bene regent.

Exercise 4.5

Translate into Latin:

1 We love the woman who gave presents to us yesterday.

2 We watch the soldiers whom the chief is leading into the country.

3 The leader has led his companions into very great danger on behalf of his country.

4 He was reading the book which you gave to me yesterday.

5 We will stand near the wall which the citizens have built.

6 The chief, whom we had led to Rome, was killed by the guards during the night.

7 We believe the new master who has punished the slaves.

8 After the citizens had departed, the enemy approached the city.

9 The old men, who were not terrified by the enemy, remained in the town.

10 The Roman soldiers will reply to the brave chief within five days.

Read the following passage and answer the questions below:

Honour is rewarded

dum Rōmānī cum <u>Pyrrhō</u> bellum gerunt, cīvis <u>Graecus</u> captus est. mox ad ducem
Rōmānum, nōmine Fabricium, vēnit et 'multam pecūniam mihi dā,' inquit. 'tum
rēgem Pyrrhum, quī vōs superāre vult, adībō et eum interficiam.'
verba tamen cīvis eius Fabricium nōn mōvērunt. 'armīs,' inquit 'nōn <u>perfidiā</u>,
5 Rōmānī hostēs superābunt.' tum custōdī quī prope eum stābat, 'discēde,' inquit
'et omnia rēgī Graecō nārrā!' custōs ad <u>castra</u> Graecōrum festīnāvit et rēgem
petīvit. eī nārrāvit, <u>sīcut</u> ā Fabriciō iussus erat, omnia quae cīvis <u>scelestus</u> dīxerat.
Pyrrhus, quī magnopere virtūte Rōmānōrum mōtus est, eōs laudāvit. multōs
autem <u>captīvōs</u>, quī in bellō captī erant, eīs <u>reddidit</u>.

Pyrrhus, -ī, m. = Pyrrhus (King of Epirus in Greece)	sīcut = just as
Graecus, -a, -um = Greek	scelestus, -a, -um = wicked
perfidia, -ae, f. = treachery	captīvus, -ī, m. = prisoner
castra, -ōrum, n. pl. = camp	reddō, reddere, reddidī, redditum = I give back

1 dum Rōmānī ... gerunt (line 1). What were the Romans doing?

2 cīvis Graecus captus est (line 1). What do we learn about the Greek citizen?

3 mox ad ... vēnit (lines 1–2). Where did the Greek citizen go then?

4 'multam pecūniam ... interficiam' (lines 2–3). What did the citizen ask for
and what did he offer to do?

5 verba tamen ... nōn mōvērunt (line 4). How did Fabricius react?

6 'armīs ... superābunt' (lines 4–5). What point was Fabricius making with
these words?

7 tum custōdī ... nārrā!' (lines 5–6). What instructions did Fabricius give?

8 eī nārrāvit ... dīxerat (line 7). What did the guard do when he found Pyrrhus?

9 Pyrrhus ... laudavit (line 8). How did Pyrrhus react?

10 multōs ... reddidit (lines 8–9). How did Pyrrhus demonstrate his admiration
for the way the Romans behaved in this episode?

Exercise 4.7

Translate into Latin:

1 The soldier, who was fighting bravely, has been wounded.

2 She has been warned by the cruel master, whom she fears.

3 Wine has been carried to the town which is near the river.

4 They have been killed by the slaves who live in the city.

5 The old man who lives on the island had been carried across the river.

Exercise 4.8

Translate into English:

1 dux, quī hostēs superāvit, cum mīlitibus audāciōribus pugnābat.

2 prīnceps, quī multās gentēs regēbat, Rōmam contendere ā rēge coāctus est.

3 quattuor diēs et trēs noctēs tempestāte territī erant.

4 multa tēla in hostēs, quī flūmen adībant, iacta sunt.

5 cīvēs rēgī, quod patriam semper amāverat, crēdidērunt.

6 septem amīcī, quī prope montēs habitābant, in urbe convēnērunt.

7 senex per viās urbis lentē ambulābat.

8 intereā ancillae, quae ā prīncipe territae erant, cibum et vīnum parābant.

9 iuvenis, quī fīlius deī erat, līberōs suōs in somnō interfēcit.

10 prīnceps in proeliō saevō paene interfectus est.

Exercise 4.9

Read the following passage and answer the questions below.

The labours of Hercules: the Stymphalian birds, the Cretan bull and the horses of Diomedes

Herculēs ab Eurystheō <u>avēs</u> <u>Stymphālidēs</u> interficere iussus est. hae <u>rōstra aēnea</u> habēbant et <u>carnem hūmānam</u> edēbant. Herculēs, postquam ad locum adiit, <u>lacum</u>, in quō <u>avēs</u> habitābant, cōnspēxit. <u>lacus plēnus līmī</u> erat nec hominēs poterant ibi nāvigāre nec ambulāre. Herculēs igitur auxilium ā deā Minervā
5   petīvit. illa eī <u>crotalum</u> ex <u>aere fabricātum</u> dedit. <u>crotalō</u> Herculēs <u>crepitum</u> maximum fēcit et <u>avēs</u> terruit. in caelum <u>volābant</u> et multae sagittīs Herculis <u>trānsfīxae</u> sunt.

posteā Herculēs Crētam contendit et <u>taurum</u>, quī agrōs <u>vastābant</u>, cēpit. inde in Thrāciam, ubi rēx, nōmine Diomēdēs, equōs saevōs habēbat, missus est.

10 Diomēdēs omnēs, quī in eam <u>regiōnem</u> vēnerant, eīs equīs <u>obiciēbant</u>. equī enim <u>carnem</u> <u>hūmānam</u> edēbant. Herculēs autem rēgem adiit. 'dā mihi eōs equōs,' inquit. 'nōlī <u>hospitēs</u> tuōs eīs <u>obicere</u>!' rēx tamen <u>pārēre</u> nōluit et cum Hercule pugnābat. rēx interfectus est et ab Hercule equīs <u>obiectus est</u>. inde equī in nāvem pulsī sunt et Herculēs cum eīs ad Eurystheum <u>rediit</u>.

avis, -is, f. = bird	fabricātus, -a, -um = made
Stymphālidēs = Stymphalian	crepitus (acc. crepitum), m. = a noise
rōstrum, -ī, n. = beak	volō, -āre = I fly
aēneus, -a, -um = brazen	trānsfīgō, -ere, -fīxī, -fīxum = I pierce
carō, carnem, f. = flesh	taurus, -ī, m. = bull
hūmānus, -a, -um = human	vastō, -āre = I ravage
lacus (acc. lacum), m. = a lake	regiō, -ōnis, f. = region
plēnus, -a, -um = full	obiciō, -ere, obiēcī, obiectum = I throw to
līmus, -ī, m. = mud	hospes, -itis, m. = guest
crotalum, -ī, n. = castanet	pāreō, -ēre (+ dat.) = I obey
aes, aeris, n. = bronze	redeō, -īre, rediī, reditum = I return

1 From the first paragraph, give and translate one example of each of the following:

(a) a verb in the perfect passive

(c) a superlative adjective

(b) a preposition followed by the accusative case

(d) a present infinitive active.

2 cōnspēxit (line 3). Which tense of which verb is this?

3 poterant (line 4). Which tense of which verb is this?

4 petīvit (line 5). Explain the connection between this Latin word and the English word **petition**.

5 eī (line 5). In which case is this word? What is its nominative singular masculine form?

6 dedit (line 5). Put this verb into the future tense, keeping the person and number the same.

7 fēcit (line 6). Which tense of which verb is this?

8 Translate the second paragraph into English.

Vocabulary 4

Latin	English
Verbs	
adeō, adīre, adiī, aditum	I approach
contendō, contendere, contendī, contentum	I hurry, march, strive
conveniō, -īre, convēnī, conventum	I meet, come together
crēdō, -ere, crēdidī, crēditum + dat.	I trust, believe
Nouns	
gēns, gentis, f.	people, race
somnus, -ī, m.	sleep
tēlum, -ī, n.	spear, missile
Adverbs	
intereā	meanwhile
lentē	slowly
paene	almost
Relative pronoun	
quī, quae, quod	who, which

Caratacus

We learnt above about how the Greek king Pyrrhus was impressed by the way the Romans behaved in war. A few hundred years later, it was the Romans who were to be impressed.

> This topic is part of the Non-Linguistic Studies section of the ISEB syllabus.

After Claudius invaded Britain in AD 43, Caratacus, the king of the Catuvellauni, put up a strong resistance to the invading force of the Romans. He defended Camulodunum (Colchester) until it eventually fell, and then fled into Wales to continue the fight against the Romans. Eventually he was defeated in battle near the River Severn by the Roman commander Ostorius Scapula and he sought refuge among the Brigantes, a tribe in the north of Britain. However, the queen of the Brigantes handed Caratacus over to the Romans and he was sent back to Rome, where he was forced to march through the city in chains as part of a triumph. Caratacus knew that he was going to be killed, but he showed no fear, and Claudius was so impressed with his bravery that he spared him and welcomed him and his family into his household as honoured guests.

Exercise 4.10

(a) (i) Tell the story of Caratacus.

(ii) What was it about the British king that impressed Claudius?

(b) (i) How did Hercules deal with either the Stymphalian birds or the horses of Diomedes?

(ii) Which of these two labours would you consider to have been the more difficult and why?

■ The major roads, towns and tribes of Roman Britain

5 The irregular verb ferō; alius, ipse and īdem

◯ Irregular verb: ferō

ferō, ferre, tulī, lātum = I carry, bear	
Active	Passive
Present	
ferō	feror
fers	ferris
fert	fertur
ferimus	ferimur
fertis	feriminī
ferunt	feruntur
Future	
feram	ferar
ferēs	ferēris
feret	ferētur
ferēmus	ferēmur
ferētis	ferēminī
ferent	ferentur
Imperfect	
ferēbam	ferēbar
ferēbās	ferēbāris
ferēbat	ferēbātur
ferēbāmus	ferēbāmur
ferēbātis	ferēbāminī
ferēbant	ferēbantur

The principal parts of this verb are rather peculiar, but the tenses formed on the perfect and supine stems are formed in a perfectly regular way, as is the case for all verbs, however irregular.

tulī = I have carried
tuleram = I had carried
lātus sum = I have been carried
lātus eram = I had been carried
Other forms to note:
Imperatives: fer, ferte
Present infinitive passive: ferrī

Exercise 5.1

Study the information above about ferō. Then, revising your irregular verbs, translate into Latin, using possum, eō or ferō:

1 He is able.

2 They were carrying.

3 They will be able.

4 We are being carried.

5 You (sing.) are carrying.

6 It will be borne.

7 We were going.

8 We were not able.

9 She will go.

10 I shall be able.

Exercise 5.2

Translate into English:

1 adeunt.

2 inībant.

3 potestis.

4 ferre.

5 poterāmus.

6 exit.

7 posse.

8 feriminī.

9 ferēminī.

10 adīre.

Exercise 5.3

Translate into Latin, using ferō, not portō, where appropriate:

1 They have carried.

2 You (sing.) have gone.

3 She has been able.

4 We have carried.

5 You (pl.) had gone out.

6 They had carried.

7 I (feminine) have been carried.

8 He had carried.

9 You (sing.) have gone in.

10 They have gone back.

alius = other

The Latin for 'other' is alius, alia, aliud, e.g. with another friend = cum aliō amīcō.

	M	F	N
Nom.	alius	alia	aliud
Acc.	alium	aliam	aliud
Gen.	alius*	alius*	alius*
Dat.	aliī**	aliī**	aliī**
Abl.	aliō	aliā	aliō
Nom.	aliī	aliae	alia
Acc.	aliōs	aliās	alia
Gen.	aliōrum	aliārum	aliōrum
Dat.	aliīs	aliīs	aliīs
Abl.	aliīs	aliīs	aliīs

*alterius, the gen. sing. of alter (see below), is normally used in place of alius.

**alterī, the dat. sing. of alter (see below), is normally used in place of aliī.

Go further

alter = other (of two)

If 'other' refers to the 'other *of two*' (e.g. the other leg), then alter is used rather than alius:

	M	F	N
Nom.	alter	altera	alterum
Acc.	alterum	alteram	alterum
Gen.	alterīus	alterīus	alterīus
Dat.	alterī	alterī	alterī
Abl.	alterō	alterā	alterō
Nom.	alterī	alterae	altera
Acc.	alterōs	alterās	altera
Gen.	alterōrum	alterārum	alterōrum
Dat.	alterīs	alterīs	alterīs
Abl.	alterīs	alterīs	alterīs

> ### aliī ... aliī
>
> A very common use of the adjective alius is in the phrase aliī ... aliī meaning some ... others.
>
> E.g.   aliī dormiēbant, aliī legēbant = Some were sleeping, others were reading.
>
>   aliōs capiēbant, aliōs interficiēbant = They were capturing some, killing others.

Exercise 5.4

Translate into English:

1 crās aquam ad mūrōs magnōs ferent.

2 herī cibum ad alterum fīlium ducis ferēbātis.

3 mīlitēs Rōmānī aliam urbem capere nōn poterant.

4 prīnceps arma in oppidum celeriter ferre poterat.

5 nōnne in urbem redībis et aquam ad alterum templum portābis?

6 aliī in templō cantābant, aliī in viā currēbant.

7 quis alteram sorōrem tuam gladiō vulnerāvit?

8 senex miser in oppidum ab iuvene lātus est.

9 propter perīcula bellī tēla ā mīlitibus ferēbantur.

10 rēgīna aliam ancillam pūnīre nōn cupiēbat.

Exercise 5.5

Translate into Latin:

1 The young man was able to carry the weapons for a long time.

2 We will soon approach another temple of the goddess.

3 Were you carrying arms to the Roman soldiers?

4 Money was being brought for the children of the king.

5 Are you able to overcome the other* king, soldiers?

6 Some were carrying food, others were carrying water.

7 He will go to the river because he cannot carry water.

8 The gifts have been carried across the river by the slave.

9 He feared the storms because he was not able to sail to the island.

10 The arrows had been carried by the soldier who was fighting bravely.

* other of two

⃝ ipse and īdem

ipse = 'self' is an **intensive pronoun**, while īdem = 'the same' is a **definitive pronoun**.

E.g. The women themselves = fēminae ipsae.

E.g. The same women = fēminae eaedem.

Ipse and īdem decline as follows:

ipse, ipsa, ipsum = self			
	M	**F**	**N**
Nom.	ipse	ipsa	ipsum
Acc.	ipsum	ipsam	ipsum
Gen.	ipsius	ipsius	ipsius
Dat.	ipsī	ipsī	ipsī
Abl.	ipsō	ipsā	ipsō
Nom.	ipsī	ipsae	ipsa
Acc.	ipsōs	ipsās	ipsa
Gen.	ipsōrum	ipsārum	ipsōrum
Dat.	ipsīs	ipsīs	ipsīs
Abl.	ipsīs	ipsīs	ipsīs

īdem, eadem, idem = the same			
	M	**F**	**N**
Nom.	īdem	eadem	idem
Acc.	eundem	eandem	idem
Gen.	eiusdem	eiusdem	eiusdem
Dat.	eīdem	eīdem	eīdem
Abl.	eōdem	eādem	eōdem
Nom.	eīdem/īdem	eaedem	eadem
Acc.	eōsdem	eāsdem	eadem
Gen.	eōrundem	eārundem	eōrundem
Dat.	eīsdem*	eīsdem*	eīsdem*
Abl.	eīsdem*	eīsdem*	eīsdem*

*or īsdem.

Exercise 5.6

Study the information above about ipse and īdem. Then translate:

1 quis custōdiet ipsōs custōdēs?

2 eīdem mīlitēs iterum pugnābunt.

3 rēx ipse in proelium festīnāvit.

4 pecūnia ā servīs eīsdem lāta est.

5 urbēs ab eōdem rēge regēbantur.

6 dux ipse cēterōs mīlitēs pūnīvit.

7 prīnceps labōrem eōrundem custōdum semper laudāvit.

8 mulier ipsa dōnum virō dedit.

9 nautae ipsī nāvem parvam trāns montēs tulērunt.

10 in proeliō mīles ā duce ipsō interfectus est.

Exercise 5.7

Read the following passage and answer the questions below.

The end of the first Punic War, 242 BC

postquam Rēgulus Carthāginem rediit, Poenī bellum cum Rōmānīs iterum
gerēbant. imperātōrem, nōmine Hamilcarem, in Siciliam mīsērunt. ille autem
victōriās prope montēs Herctem et Erycem mox peperit. Rōmānī
igitur cōpiās trāns īnsulam dūxērunt et cum hostibus pugnāvērunt. Poenī
5 paucissimōs mīlitēs habēbant sed diū Rōmānōrum impetūs sustinēre poterant.
tandem tamen Rōmānī classem parāvērunt et Poenōs, quī multās nāvēs
domum iam mīserant, prope Drepana superāvērunt. Poenī victī sunt et pācem
petīvērunt. ē Siciliā discessērunt nec post hoc proelium rediērunt.

Carthāgō, -inis, f. = Carthage	Herctēs, Herctis, m. = Mt. Hercte
Poenī, -ōrum, m. pl. = the Carthaginians	Eryx, Erycis, m. = Mt. Eryx
	impetūs (acc. pl.) = the attacks
imperātor, -ōris, m. = general	sustineō, -ēre = I withstand
Hamilcar, -aris, m. = Hamilcar	classis, -is, f. = fleet
victōriam pariō, -ere, peperī = I win a victory	domum (acc.) = (to) home
	Drepana, -ōrum, n. pl. = Drepana

1 postquam ... gerēbant (lines 1–2). When did the Carthaginians start fighting with the Romans again?

2 imperātōrem ... mīsērunt (line 2). Who was Hamilcar?

3 victōriās ... pugnāvērunt (lines 3–4). What happened following Hamilcar's arrival in Sicily? Make at least three points.

4 Poenī ... poterant (lines 4–5). Why was it surprising that the Carthaginians withstood the Roman attacks?

5 tandem ... superāvērunt (lines 6–7). Explain what happened at Drepana.

6 Poenī ... rediērunt (lines 7–8). What effect did this have on the outcome of the war?

7 rediit (line 1). Which part of which verb is this?

8 gerēbant (line 2). Put this verb into the future tense, keeping the person and number the same. Give the supine of this verb.

9 ille (line 2). What type of word is this? What would it be if it were accusative singular, neuter?

10 īnsulam (line 4). In which case is this word, and why?

11 paucissimōs (line 5). What form of the adjective is this?

12 poterant (line 5). Which part of which verb is this?

13 quī (line 6). What type of word is this? What would it be if it were accusative plural, neuter?

14 pācem (line 7). Explain the connection between this Latin word and the English word **pacify**.

15 Translate the passage into English.

---

quam + superlative

The phrase 'as ... as possible' is translated into Latin by quam + a superlative.

E.g.   quam celerrimē = as quickly as possible.

         quam fortissimē = as bravely as possible.

Can you do possum?

Remember, the Latin verb possum = I am able is used to translate the English verb 'can'.

E.g.   I can run = currere possum.

Exercise 5.8

Study the information above. Then translate into Latin:

1 The king himself can punish the citizens.

2 The leader watched his soldiers for five days.

3 We will fight as bravely as possible.

4 Regulus himself did not fear the enemy.

5 We cannot bear the anger of the gods.

6 No one can help the son of the guard.

7 He can always give tasks to the same slaves.

8 The courage of the mother was greater than that of her son.

9 We shall go as quickly as possible towards the city.

10 The soldiers can attack another town.

Exercise 5.9

Using the words from Vocabularies 1–5, say from which Latin words the following English ones derive. Translate the Latin word and explain the meaning of the English one:

1	Annual	6	Fidelity
2	Accelerator	7	Nocturnal
3	Convention	8	Principal
4	Laborious	9	Tempestuous
5	Custody	10	Insomnia

Translating passages of English into Latin is no harder, really, than translating a series of sentences. This is called prose composition and is a very good test of how well you are getting on with your Latin.

Exercise 5.10

Translate into Latin:

For many years the Roman forces waged war with the peoples of Italy. Once, a Greek king, called Pyrrhus, came to Italy with many soldiers. He brought help to the enemies of Rome, but in vain. After this the Romans feared the forces of Carthage and wanted to overcome them. Regulus led his soldiers into Africa but was captured. Then the war was waged in Sicily again. But at last the leader of the Carthaginians, called Hamilcar, was forced to fight with the Romans by sea and was defeated.

people = gēns, gentis, f.	Africa = Āfrica, -ae, f.
Italy = Ĭtalia, -ae, f.	the war was waged = pugnātum est
Rome = Rōma, -ae, f.	Carthaginians = Poenī, -ōrum, m. pl.
Carthage = Carthāgō, -inis, f.	

Exercise 5.11

Read the following passage and answer the questions that follow.

The labours of Hercules: the girdle of Hippolyte

Hippolytē, rēgīna <u>Amāzonum</u>, <u>balteum</u> pulcherrimum, quem deus Mars eī dederat, habēbat. Admēta, fīlia Eurystheī, magnopere <u>balteum</u> illum cupiēbat. Eurystheus igitur Herculem in terram <u>Amāzonum</u> mīsit. 'balteum rēgīnae cape,' inquit, 'et ad mē quam celerrimē fer!'

5 Herculēs multōs sociōs collēgit et in <u>fīnēs Amāzonum</u> nāvigāvit. nūntium ad rēgīnam mīsit et <u>balteum popōscit</u>. rēgīna dē Hercule multa audīverat et <u>balteum</u> eī trādere volēbat. cēterae tamen <u>Amāzonēs</u> īrātissimae erant et bellum Herculī et sociīs eius <u>indīxērunt</u>.

diū et ācriter pugnātum est. mulierēs fortiter pugnābant et cōpiās Herculis īn
10 fugam pepulērunt. hic tamen comitēs admonuit. 'nōlīte fūgere,' inquit. 'nōnne
fēminās superāre et balteum capere possumus? in proelium redīte!'

tandem cōpiae Herculis Amāzonas vīcērunt et rēgīnam eārum occīdērunt.
balteum cēpērunt et in nāvem rediērunt.

Amāzones, -onum (acc. = Amazonas), f. pl. = the Amazons	indīcō, -ere, indīxī, indictum = I declare (war)
balteus, -ī, m. = belt, girdle	ācriter = fiercely
fīnēs, -um, m. pl. = territory	fuga, -ae, f. = flight
pōscō, -ere, popōscī = I demand, ask for	admoneō, -ēre = I admonish

1 Hippolytē ... habēbat (lines 1–2). What had Mars given to Hippolyte?

2 Admēta ... cupiēbat (line 2). What did Admeta think of the gift?

3 Eurystheus ... fer!' (lines 3–4). How did Admeta's father respond to this situation?

4 Herculēs ... nāvigāvit (line 5). How did Hercules prepare before setting out on his expedition?

5 nūntium ... popōscit (lines 5–6). What did he do when he arrived in the territory of the Amazons?

6 rēgīna ... volēbat (lines 6–7). What was Hippolyte's initial response to the message?

7 cēterae ... indīxērunt (lines 7–8). Did the other Amazons share her view? Explain your answer.

8 pugnātum est (line 9). In which tense and voice is this verb? What does it mean literally, and how might you translate it into more natural language?

9 mulierēs (line 9). In which case is this noun?

10 pepulērunt (line 10). Which part of which verb is this?

11 admonuit (line 10).

(a) Give the Latin subject of this verb.

(b) Give the Latin object of this verb.

12 nōlīte fūgere (line 10). Translate this phrase into English.

13 possumus (line 11).

(a) Which part of which verb is this?

(b) What would it become in the imperfect tense?

14 redīte (line 11). Which part of which verb is this?

15 vīcērunt (line 12).

(a) Give the Latin subject of this verb.

(b) Give the Latin object of this verb.

16 nāvem (line 13). In which case is this word, and why?

17 Translate the passage into English.

Vocabulary 5

Latin	English
Pronouns	
alius, alia, aliud	other
īdem, eadem, idem	the same
ipse, ipsa, ipsum	self
Verbs	
ferō, ferre, tulī, lātum (irreg.)	I carry, bear
iuvō, iuvāre, iūvī, iūtum	I help

Roman villas

When the Romans began to establish themselves in Britain, following the invasion of Claudius in AD 43, they built roads to connect the main strategic centres, camps in which to house their troops, and towns. But a new form of housing also began to be seen, based on the country homes of Romans back in Italy: villas. Some of these were relatively small buildings, built around a farm, but many were constructed on much grander lines, often to impress. A good example of such a villa is the one built at Fishbourne, near Chichester, probably for the ruler of the Atrebates, Cogidubnus, in around AD 75. These grand villas would have had several reception rooms, gardens, baths, all decorated in the Roman style with mosaic floors and frescoes on the walls.

> This topic is part of the Non-Linguistic Studies section of the ISEB syllabus.

■ A model of the Roman villa at Fishbourne showing how it looked originally

Exercise 5.12

(a) (i) What happened when Hercules was sent to get the girdle of Hippolyte?

(ii) Do you think Hercules's men were surprised by what happened when they began to fight the Amazons, and if so, why?

(b) (i) Draw a sketch of a typical Roman villa, labelling the main rooms.

(ii) How might such a building have been used in Roman Britain to demonstrate the power of the Romans?

6 Participles

Participles are adjectives formed from verbs. Like normal adjectives, they agree with the noun or pronoun they describe in gender, case and number. In Latin there are three participles: present, future and past. We shall begin with the present participle.

Present participle

Present participles (which in English end in '-ing') are formed in Latin from the present stem, are always active, and decline like ingēns. amō and moneō add -ns to the present stem, the others add -ēns. Here they are, with their genitive singular forms:

amā-ns,	monē-ns,	reg-ēns,	audi-ēns,	capi-ēns,
amantis	monentis	regentis	audientis	capientis
loving	warning	ruling	hearing	taking

	M	F	N
Nom.	amāns	amāns	amāns
Acc.	amantem	amantem	amāns
Gen.	amantis	amantis	amantis
Dat.	amantī	amantī	amantī
Abl.	amantī	amantī	amantī
Nom.	amantēs	amantēs	amantia
Acc.	amantēs	amantēs	amantia
Gen.	amantium	amantium	amantium
Dat.	amantibus	amantibus	amantibus
Abl.	amantibus	amantibus	amantibus

Present participles may be said to describe what the nouns with which they agree are 'doing'.

E.g. The girl watched her mother *walking* in the garden =
      puella mātrem in hortō ambulantem spectābat.

In this example, the participle 'walking' stands in place of a phrase such as *while she was walking* and thus tells us what the mother was doing.

When translating from Latin, it is often possible to use a clause to represent a present participle. This could be a temporal clause, giving an indication of time, but might also be a relative clause, adding further information.

E.g. hostēs arma ferentēs timēmus = We fear the enemy *when* they bear arms.

OR We fear the enemy *who are* bearing arms.

Irregular participles

Most present participles are easy enough to form from the present stem, but the odd problem crops up here and there with the irregular verbs:

ferō: ferēns, ferentis. (Surprisingly, this is completely regular!)

eō: iēns, euntis. (This, by contrast, is very silly!)

possum: potēns, potentis exists as an adjective (= 'powerful') but must *not* be used as a participle.

sum: no participle exists. There is, thus, no Latin word for 'being'.

Take care with that very silly-looking participle from eō.

E.g. We watched the boy going into the field = puerum spectāvimus in agrum euntem.

Exercise 6.1

Study the information above about present participles. Give the nominative masculine singular and genitive masculine singular of the following participles:

1 Calling

2 Fighting

3 Remaining

4 Reading

5 Going

6 Handing over

7 Helping

8 Conquering

9 Seeking

10 Driving

Exercise 6.2

Translate into English:

1 nāvēs in flūmen nāvigantēs spectābat.

2 mīlitēs virōs Rōmānōs in templō sedentēs vīdērunt.

3 puerī equum prope mūrum stantem cēpērunt.

4 ducem Rōmānum mīlitēs in proelium dūcentem spectābāmus.

5   poētam in agrō cantantem audīvī.

6   Troiānī Graecōs dōna ferentēs nōn timēbant.

7   servus dominum in agrōs ineuntem vīdit.

8   tempestās gentēs in montibus habitantēs terruit.

9   prīnceps ā fēminīs ē templō festīnantibus vīsus est.

10 prīnceps ā fēminīs ē templō festīnāns vīsus est.

Exercise 6.3

Translate into Latin. Always be sure to make the participle agree with the noun or pronoun to which it refers.

1   We watched the boys running into the field.

2   Sitting near the wall, the farmer watched the slaves.

3   The farmer watched the slaves sitting near the wall.

4   The proud leader praised the fighting soldiers.

5   The schoolmaster was reading a book, sitting near the boys and girls.

6   No one likes the master of the sleeping girl.

7   The slaves will not overcome the fighting Romans, will they?

8   Why have the women left the boy sleeping in the field?

9   The leader, while returning from the battle, gave a reward to his soldiers.

10 The leader gave a reward to his soldiers, (while they were) returning from the battle.

Using Latin

Sometimes, when learning complicated rules about Latin, it is hard to believe that the Romans ever actually spoke this language. But they did. And while we are learning about present participles, here is one of the most famous phrases in Latin, from the Roman poet, Virgil:

timeō Danaōs et dōna ferentēs.

I fear the Greeks, even when bearing gifts. (Virgil, *Aeneid* 2.49)

Danaus is a word for Greek, and the quotation refers to the time during the Trojan War when the Greeks tricked the Trojans into taking the wooden horse into the city. Notice, also, how the word et can mean 'even' as well as 'and'.

Go further

Present participles and English spelling

It is a well-known fact that English spelling is difficult. How, for example, would you explain to a Martian that the words 'plough', 'enough', and 'through' – which sound completely different – are spelt in the same way?

But Latin is often there in the background, easing our way through these little minefields. And, now that you have met present participles, there is a whole range of English words which you stand a pretty good chance of spelling correctly, namely those ending in -ent, -ant, -ence or -ance. Take the following:

- Ambulance
- Convenience
- Repellent
- Audience
- Credence
- Repugnant

The difficulty with words such as these is knowing which vowel to use before the n; is it an *a* or an *e*? The following principle won't always work, I'm afraid, but it's pretty good. When in doubt, think about which Latin verb is involved, and then look at that verb's present participle. Thus ambulance, from ambulāns; audience from audiēns; and so on.

Of course, there is a problem with this. Some words in -ant have come to us via French, rather than directly from Latin. Thus the word 'descendant' has come from the French *descendre*, with its participle *descendant*, not dēscendō with its participle dēscendēns. And the word 'servant', which looks from its spelling as though it comes from the Latin servō, servāre = 'I save' in fact comes from serviō, servīre = 'I serve' and thus has no business being spelt with an *a*. Again, this is because it comes to us via the participle of the French *servir*, i.e. *servant*.

The study of where words come from in this way is called etymology.

Exercise 6.4

Study the information above about participles and English spelling. Translate and then give an English word derived from the following Latin participles. In all cases the most common mis-spelling involves the *a* or *e* near the end of the word:

1 cōnstituēns

2 currēns

3 ambulāns

4 occupāns

5 audiēns

6 respondēns

7 cōgēns

8 crēdēns

9 repellēns

10 exspectāns

Exercise 6.5

Translate into English the following story, which is adapted from one of Aesop's fables:

agricola quīnque fīliōs habuit. fīliī saepe <u>disputābant</u> nec bene labōrābant. pater igitur <u>fascem</u> ūnī fīliō dedit et 'potesne' inquit 'hunc <u>fascem</u> <u>frangere</u>?' puer fascem <u>frangere</u> nōn potuit. tum pater <u>fascem</u> aliō fīliō dedit. 'potesne tū' inquit pater 'hunc <u>fascem</u> <u>frangere</u>?' nōn potuit. mox omnēs puerī <u>fascem</u> <u>frangere</u> <u>temptāverant</u> sed frūstrā. deinde agricola <u>fascem</u> <u>solvit</u> et <u>virgās</u> <u>singulās</u> fīliīs spectantibus dedit. puerī <u>virgās</u> <u>facile</u> <u>frēgērunt</u>. inde pater rīdēns 'sōlī' inquit 'validī nōn estis. <u>ūnā</u> tamen vōs ā nūllō superābiminī!'

> disputō, -āre, -āvī, -ātum = I argue
> fascis, fascis, m. = a bundle of sticks
> frangō, -ere, frēgī, frāctum = I break
> temptō, -āre, -āvī, -ātum = I try
> solvō, solvere, solvī, solūtum = I untie
> virga, -ae, f. = stick
> singulī -ae, -a = one at a time
> facile = easily
> ūnā (adv.) = together

Exercise 6.6

Translate into Latin:

1 A farmer was working in his fields, preparing the land.

2 'You aren't able,' he said, 'to conquer all your brothers, are you?'

3 The boy, holding a sword, ran towards his brothers.

4 The angry father did not praise his fighting sons.

5 'You are strong' he said, 'but, fighting alone, you cannot overcome your enemies.'

Exercise 6.7

Translate into English:

1 omnēs timēbant, in oppidum festīnantēs.

2 iuvenis sorōrem prope flūmen sedentem invēnit.

3 nōnne nāvēs ad īnsulam nāvigantēs spectāre cupis?

4 dux hostium mīlitēs suōs urbem oppugnantēs spectāvit.

5 quis cīvēs rēgīnam laudantēs cōnspexit?

Perfect participle passive

As you already know, the perfect participle passive, or PPP as it likes to be called, is formed from the supine stem and declines like bonus. So far, you have only used it as part of the perfect passive tense, but it survives perfectly well on its own.

amātus, -a, -um	(having been) loved
monitus, -a, um	(having been) warned
rēctus, -a, -um	(having been) ruled
audītus, -a, um	(having been) heard
captus, -a, um	(having been) taken

When you are getting used to the PPP, always imagine the words 'having been' in your translation and you will not go far wrong.

E.g. puellam ā mīlitibus captam vīdimus =
We saw the girl (*having been captured*) by the soldiers.
This can then be put into more natural English as follows:
We saw the girl *captured* by the soldiers; or
We saw the girl *when she had been captured* by the soldiers.

As you can see, the best translation of a PPP will almost never involve the words 'having been'. But if you translate a PPP with these words to start with, you can always put it into more natural English later, when you are certain that you know what you are doing. Above all, the most important thing to remember about the PPP is that it is *passive*. You would be amazed how many people forget this simple fact.

Study the information above about the perfect participle passive. Before translating the following sentences, bracket the PPP with the noun with which it agrees (as if it were a normal adjective). The first two are done for you. Then translate into English:

1 puer parvus (agricolam interfectum) vīdit.

2 (servus inventus) ad dominum statim missus est.

3 puella librum lēctum amīcō dedit.

4 puellam ā mātre relictam invenīre nōn poterāmus.

5 nāvis in īnsulā aedificāta tempestāte dēlēta est.

6 animālia in agrōs pulsa sagittīs occīdimus.

7 tēlum ā mīlite relictum iuvenī dedī.

8 prīnceps praemium cīvibus quīnque annōs custōdītīs dare cupiēbat.

9 spem multīs gentibus ā rēge saevō rēctīs dedimus.

10 quis pecūniam diū petitam ad templum ferēbat?

Exercise 6.9

We do not often say 'having been' in English (e.g. 'having been loved'), but this phrase is really useful for showing that a PPP is being used. Bearing this in mind, translate the following into Latin:

1 We see the horses walking into the field.

2 They saw the enemy attacking the town.

3 He led the (having been) captured slaves into the street.

4 Soldiers hurrying into battle always trust their leaders.

5 Surely the gods were not punishing the (having been) conquered citizens?

6 The young man found a beautiful girl (having been) left in the mountains.

7 The chief watched the soldiers laughing in the street with the citizens.

8 The Romans were able to wage another war against the (having been) defeated enemy.

9 The women saw the slave-girl playing near the walls of the city.

10 Having been captured by the soldiers, she was killed by their shields.

Go further

Dative of the possessor

As you know, habeō = I have, and it is very common to write a sentence such as:

puer multōs librōs habet = The boy has many books.

However, it is equally acceptable to use the dative case with the verb sum:

puerō multī librī sunt = To the boy there are many books (i.e. the boy has many books).

This construction is used, as Kennedy's *Latin Grammar* will remind you, when the emphasis is being placed on the thing possessed, not on the possessor. In the passage below, you will see an example of this, which we hope you will be able to cope with quite easily.

Exercise 6.10

Read the following passage and answer the questions below.

The labours of Hercules: the apples of the Hesperides

Herculēs, postquam <u>Amāzonas</u> superāvit et <u>balteum</u> rēgīnae cēpit, <u>bovēs</u>
<u>Gēryonis</u> ad Eurystheum dūxit. post autem hunc labōrem decimum, rēx Herculī
opus <u>gravius</u> <u>imposuit</u>. 'ad mē,' inquit, '<u>aurea</u> <u>māla</u> quae in <u>hortō</u>
<u>Hesperidum</u> custōdiuntur.' <u>dracō</u> enim, cui centum capita erant, haec māla in hortō
5 custōdiēbat.
Herculēs per multās terrās iter fēcit nec tamen <u>hortum Hesperidum</u> invenīre
poterat. tandem ad <u>extrēmam</u> partem <u>orbis</u> terrārum <u>pervēnit</u>. hīc virum ingentem,
nōmine <u>Atlantem</u>, qui caelum <u>umerīs</u> suīs <u>sustinēbat</u>, cōnspexit. <u>Atlās</u>, quod
<u>Hesperidum</u> pater erat, iuvenem iuvāre volēbat. 'ego ad <u>hortum</u> ībō,' inquit, 'et
10 <u>māla</u> ā fīliābus meīs accipiam.' Herculēs laetissimus erat. <u>Atlās</u> caelum eī dedit et,
dum in <u>umerīs</u> Herculēs <u>sustinet</u>, ipse ad <u>hortum</u> festīnāvit. ibi fīliās salūtāvit et
quīntō diē <u>māla</u> ab eīs accepta ad Herculem <u>rettulit</u>. hic <u>Atlantem</u> magnō cum <u>gaudiō</u>
laudāvit et ad Graeciam rediit.

Amāzones, -onum (acc. = Amazonas), f. pl. = the Amazons	Hesperides, -um, f. pl. = the Hesperides (nymphs who tended a garden for the golden apples; daughters of Atlas)
balteus, -ī, m. = belt, girdle	
bōs, bovis, c. = ox, cow	dracō, -ōnis, m. = dragon
Gēryōn, -onis, m. = Geryon (a king with three bodies)	extrēmus, -a, -um = furthest
	orbis, -is, m. (orbis terrārum) = the world
gravis, -e = heavy, severe	perveniō, -īre = I reach
impōnō, -ere, imposuī + dat. = I impose on	Atlās, Atlantis, m. = Atlas
	umerus, -ī, m. = shoulder
aureus, -a, -um = golden	sustineō, -ēre = I hold up
mālum, -ī, n. = apple	referō, referre, rettulī, relātum = I bring back
hortus, -ī, m. = garden	gaudium, -ī, n. = joy

1 Herculēs ... dūxit (lines 1–2). What do we learn about the labours of Hercules in these lines?

2 post autem ... decimum (line 2). How many labours had Hercules undertaken at this stage?

3 rēx Herculī opus gravius imposuit (lines 2–3). What are we told about the next labour that the king set for Hercules?

4 'fer mihi ... custōdiuntur.' (lines 3–4). What were Eurystheus's instructions to Hercules?

5 dracō ... custōdiēbat (lines 4–5). Why was this a particularly challenging task?

6 Herculēs per multās terrās iter fēcit (line 6). What are we told about Hercules in this line?

7 nec tamen ... poterat (lines 6–7). What was the result of Hercules's travels?

8 tandem ... pervēnit (line 7). Where did Hercules end up eventually?

9 hīc virum ingentem ... cōnspexit (lines 7–8). Whom did he see when he got there, and what was he doing?

10 Atlās ... iuvāre volēbat (lines 8–9). Why was Atlas willing to help Hercules?

11 ego ... accipiam (lines 9–10). What offer did Atlas make?

12 Atlās caelum ... ad hortum festīnāvit (lines 10–11). Describe what happened in these lines.

13 ibi fīliās ... rettulit (lines 11–12). What did Atlas do when he went to the garden and how long was he away?

14 hic Atlantem ... rediit (lines 12–13). How did Hercules respond and what did he do next?

15 Translate the passage into English.

Go further

Using participles

As we have seen, one of the cleverest things you can do with a participle is to cut out the need for a separate clause. Examine the following examples.

> The farmer *was sitting* under a tree and *was reading* a book.

One of the verbs in italics can be changed into a participle:

> The farmer, sitting under a tree, was reading a book =

> agricola sub arbore **sedēns** librum legēbat.

This is even more impressive when we use perfect participles:

The farmer *captured* the slave and *killed* him.

This can be changed by substituting a participle for the first verb:

The farmer killed the having been captured slave =

agricola servum **captum** interfēcit.

When translating from Latin you obviously do this in reverse:

prīnceps servōs **captōs** Rōmam dūxit =

The chief led the having been captured slaves to Rome.

This then becomes:

The chief captured the slaves and led them to Rome.

◯ Volō, nōlō

You have already learnt to cope with a number of irregular verbs, so the following should not give you too much trouble. As you will see, nōlō is a contraction of nōn + volō.

volō, velle, voluī = I wish, am willing	
nōlō, nōlle, nōluī = I do not wish, am unwilling	
Present	
volō	nōlō
vīs	nōn vīs
vult	nōn vult
volumus	nōlumus
vultis	nōn vultis
volunt	nōlunt
Future	
volam	nōlam
volēs	nōlēs
volet	nōlet
volēmus	nōlēmus
volētis	nōlētis
volent	nōlent

Imperfect	
volēbam	nōlēbam
volēbās	nōlēbās
volēbat	nōlēbat
volēbāmus	nōlēbāmus
volēbātis	nōlēbātis
volēbant	nōlēbant

In the perfect tense, voluī is often translated as 'I determined' and nōluī as 'I refused'.

And you have already learnt how the imperative of nōlō is used in prohibitions (negative commands):

E.g. nōlī ambulāre, Mārce = don't walk, Marcus!

E.g. nōlīte ambulāre, puerī = don't walk, boys!
(Literally these mean 'be unwilling to walk!')

Exercise 6.11

Study the information above about volō and nōlō. Then translate into Latin:

1 He wishes to help the friends.

2 They are unwilling to flee.

3 We want to remain here.

4 They will not wish to work.

5 The poet had wished to enter Rome.

6 They want to fight in the mountains.

7 Do not flee from the city, soldiers!

8 You do not wish to lead the soldiers into the mountains, do you?

9 Don't lead your soldiers into the sea!

10 Do not run towards the deep river, Marcus!

Exercise 6.12

Translate into English:

1 cum Graecīs pugnāre nōn vultis.

2 quis mēcum ad mūrum magnum īre vult?

3 cūr servī tuī in agrō labōrāre nōlēbant?

4 hae ancillae aquam ferre in urbem nōlunt.

5 cum illīs cīvibus superbīs pugnāre nōluī.

6 nōlīte occīdere senēs!

7 hoc facere nōlēbāmus.

8 cūr puella hōs librōs legere nōlēbat?

9 iter cum amīcīs facere voluit.

10 contendere cum mīlitibus nōluit.

Exercise 6.13

Translate into English:

The battle of Cannae, 216 BC

ubi Fabius dux erat, Rōmānī cum hostibus in proeliō pugnāre diū nōlēbant. sed proximō annō, cōnsilium pessimum cēpērunt. omnēs enim Poenōs vincere volēbant et tum quidem plūrimās cōpiās habēbant. nōn arte, igitur, sed vīribus, in illō bellō hostēs superāre cōnstituērunt. duŏ autem cōnsulēs, L. Aemilius Paullus
5   et M. Terentius Varrō, quī eō tempore cum Hannibale numquam pugnāverant, copiās Rōmānās ad Poenōs dūcere cōnstituērunt.

prope oppidum, nōmine Cannās, Poenī cōpiās īnstrūxērunt. in mediā aciē paucōs peditēs posuērunt. Rōmānī, ubi hoc vīdērunt, plūrimīs cum equitibus impetum maximum in mediam aciem fēcērunt. hostēs prīmō fugere vidēbantur. equitēs
10 tamen hostium circum ālās Rōmānōrum contendērunt et Rōmānōs īn fugam pepulērunt. inde ā tergō in eōs impetum fēcērunt.

mox Rōmānī superātī sunt et plūrimī sunt interfectī. post proelium, Poenī ā digitīs Rōmānōrum ānulōs captōs Carthāginem mīsērunt.

---

proximus, -a, -um = next
cōnsilium capiō = I adopt a plan
Poenī, -ōrum, m. pl. = the Carthaginians
quidem = indeed
ars, artis, f. = art, skill
vīrēs, vīrium, f. pl. = strength
cōnsul, -is, m. = consul
Cannae, -ārum, f. pl. = Cannae
īnstruō, -ere, īnstrūxī, īnstrūctum = I draw up
aciēs, aciēī, f. = battle line
pedes, peditis, m. = foot-soldier
eques, -itis, m. = horseman (in pl. = cavalry)
impetus (acc. impetum) = attack
prīmō = at first
videor (passive of videō) = I seem
āla, -ae, f. = wing (of army)
fuga, -ae, f. = flight
tergum, -ī, n. = back
digitus, -ī, m. = finger
ānulus, -ī, m. = ring
Carthāgō, -inis, f. = Carthage

Vocabulary 6

Latin	English
Noun	
praemium, -iī, n.	reward
Adjectives	
superbus, -a, -um	proud
tōtus, -a, -um (goes like ūnus)	whole
Verbs	
nōlō, nōlle, nōluī	I am not willing, do not wish
volō, velle, voluī	I am willing, wish

Boudicca

After the defeat of Caratacus, the Romans were kept busy for ten years in Wales until, in AD 60, the Iceni, a tribe in East Anglia, rose up against them. Their queen was Boudicca. On the death of her father, she had been named as his heir. However, the Romans disregarded this, stripped her of her land and raped her daughters. Joining forces with the neighbouring Trinovantes, Boudicca attacked and burned the city of Camulodunum (Colchester) and then marched on Londinium (London) and Verulamium (St Albans), sacking these two cities too.

Eventually the Roman general Suetonius Paulinus, having marched his army back from Wales, and although massively outnumbered, defeated Boudicca's forces and slaughtered up to 80,000 Britons. Boudicca committed suicide and the rebellion she had led came to an end.

> This topic is part of the Non-Linguistic Studies section of the ISEB syllabus.

Hadrian's Wall

The Roman conquest of Britain carried on following the defeat of Boudicca, but the area to the north of the country was always considered unstable, and in AD 122 the Roman Emperor Hadrian decided to build a wall from one coast to the other, from near modern-day Carlisle in the west to Newcastle in the east. This wall served to separate the tribes in the north from those more settled in the south, and represented the northern frontier of the Roman Empire. Stretching for approximately 73 miles, the wall had small fortifications every mile (milecastles), and between each milecastle there were two watchtowers. A few years later, large forts were added along the length of the wall to house garrisons of Roman soldiers. The remains of two of these forts, Housesteads and Vindolanda, can be seen today, and archaeologists have learnt a great deal about the lives of those living and working there.

> This topic is part of the Non-Linguistic Studies section of the ISEB syllabus.

■ Milecastle 39 on Hadrian's Wall, located in Northumberland

Exercise 6.14

Find out what you can about the revolt of Boudicca and Hadrian's Wall. Then answer the questions below.

(a) (i) Tell the story of how Boudicca rose up against the Romans.

 (ii) Why was Boudicca's revolt ultimately unsuccessful?

(b) (i) Draw a sketch of Hadrian's Wall, and label the main features.

 (ii) How effective a fortification do you think it was?

(c) (i) Tell the story of how Hercules succeeded in collecting the apples of the Hesperides.

 (ii) Do you think he would have succeeded without the help of Atlas?

Imperfect subjunctive; final clauses; indirect command

7

Imperfect subjunctive

The tenses you have learnt so far have all been in the **indicative mood.** The indicative is used to express facts, such as 'the farmer loves the girl' or 'the soldiers are fighting'. You are now going to step up a gear by learning about the **subjunctive mood,** which is used when we are dealing with matters which are *not* expressed as definite facts. For example, we use the subjunctive in Latin to express purpose, wishes, possibilities, etc. There are four subjunctive tenses. The way in which these are translated depends on the nature of the construction, and the first one we are going to meet is the imperfect subjunctive.

The imperfect subjunctive of a verb is really easy to form. Simply go to the present infinitive of the verb and add -m, -s, -t, etc., lengthening the preceding 'e' where necessary.

Imperfect subjunctive active				
amāre-m	monēre-m	regere-m	audīre-m	capere-m
amārē-s	monērē-s	regerē-s	audīrē-s	caperē-s
amāre-t	monēre-t	regere-t	audīre-t	capere-t
amārē-mus	monērē-mus	regerē-mus	audīrē-mus	caperē-mus
amārē-tis	monērē-tis	regerē-tis	audīrē-tis	caperē-tis
amāre-nt	monēre-nt	regere-nt	audīre-nt	capere-nt

The passive forms are also easy. Simply convert -m, -s, -t, etc. to -r, -ris, -tur as normal.

Imperfect subjunctive passive				
amāre-r	monēre-r	regere-r	audīre-r	capere-r
amārē-ris	monērē-ris	regerē-ris	audīrē-ris	caperē-ris
amārē-tur	monērē-tur	regerē-tur	audīrē-tur	caperē-tur
amārē-mur	monērē-mur	regerē-mur	audīrē-mur	caperē-mur
amārē-minī	monērē-minī	regerē-minī	audīrē-minī	caperē-minī
amāre-ntur	monēre-ntur	regere-ntur	audīre-ntur	capere-ntur

Exercise 7.1

Study the information above about the imperfect subjunctive. Then give the following forms of the imperfect subjunctive, active and passive:

1   3rd sing., portō

2   2nd sing., videō

3   1st plural, iuvō

4   2nd plural, petō

5   1st sing., custōdiō

6   3rd plural, relinquō

7   1st plural, colligō

8   2nd sing., inveniō

9   3rd sing., servō

10   1st sing., trādō

Final clauses

The first construction involving the subjunctive which you are going to meet is called a final (or purpose) clause. A final clause expresses **purpose.** It is introduced by the conjunctions ut = 'in order that', or nē = 'in order that ... not' (i.e. 'lest'), and has its verb in the subjunctive.

E.g.   I came to the city **to see my father** (i.e. *in order that I might see my father*) =
   ad urbem vēni **ut patrem vidērem**.

E.g.   I fled from the enemy **lest I be killed** (i.e. *in order that I might not be killed*) =
   ab hostibus fūgi **nē interficerer**.

Note that in English we normally use a simple infinitive for this construction, e.g. 'to see' or 'to kill', etc. Be careful not to do this in Latin.

Exercise 7.2

Study the information above about the imperfect subjunctive and final clauses. Note how the imperfect subjunctive often means *might* and is formed from the present infinitive by adding 'm' , etc. Translate into Latin:

1   To walk

2   In order that I might walk

3   To fight

4   In order that he might fight

5   To flee

6   In order that we might flee

7   To see

8   In order that you (pl.) might see

9   To leave

10   In order that they might leave

Exercise 7.3

Once you can do the imperfect subjunctive in the active, putting it into the passive is simple, using the conversion chart on page 1 (-ō/m, -s, -t, -mus, -tis, -nt becomes -or/r, -ris, -tur, -mur, -minī, -ntur). Translate into Latin, using the imperfect subjunctive:

1 In order that we might be led

2 In order that she might not be watched

3 In order that they might be killed

4 Lest I be captured

5 In order that they might be driven

6 In order that it might be read

7 In order that you (pl.) might be found

8 In order that we might be asked

9 Lest we be overcome

10 Lest it be attacked

Exercise 7.4

Study the information above about final clauses. Translate into English:

1 fēmina in agrōs festīnābat ut agricolam fessum invenīret.

2 dux Rōmānus cōpiās collēgit ut cum hostibus pugnāret.

3 Rōmā discessimus nē ā mīlitibus saevīs interficerēmur.

4 puella ut cibum parāret per viam festīnāvit.

5 ad templum veniēbant ut deōs laudārent.

6 hostēs, nē ā Rōmānīs invenīrentur, cōpiās ad flūmen dūxērunt.

7 Hannibal suōs in montēs dūxit ut in Ītaliam iter faceret.

8 mulierēs in agrōs festīnāvērunt ut ā līberīs salūtārentur.

9 ducēs, ut copiās hostium caperent, ad flūmen adiērunt.

10 num Rōmam vēnistī ut templa nova vidērēs?

Exercise 7.5

Translate into Latin. Remember that with final clauses, where in English we use a simple infinitive (e.g. 'to see'), Latin uses ut or nē plus the subjunctive.

1 We came to Rome to see your friends.

2 You departed from Rome lest you see my mother.

3 You didn't come to the city to read all my books, did you?

4 The farmer hurried into the temple lest he be killed by his brother.

5 The mother ran into the street to find her daughter.

6 The poet walked into the mountains to look at the sky.

7 The wise man placed his food near the wall lest it be found by the animals.

8 Who came to the sea to see the ships?

9 The soldiers hurried across the river to attack the city.

10 The chief came to give a reward to the brave citizen.

Go further

The sequence of tenses

There is a very important principle to learn about the way clauses fit together, called the sequence of tenses. Verbs in Latin may be either **primary** (present, future or perfect) or **historic** (imperfect, pluperfect or simple past). When joining clauses together, the general principle is that if the main verb is primary, the verb in the subordinate clause should be primary; if it is historic, the verb in the subordinate clause should be historic. You will learn more about this later, but for now, what it means is that when translating final clauses in which the verb in the subordinate clause is in the imperfect subjunctive, the main verb must be translated as a *historic* verb. So for example, amāvī would mean *I loved*, not *I have loved*.

E.g. Rōmam **vēnī** ut patrem vidērem = I **came** to Rome to see my father.

This involves making sure you understand the essential difference between the *primary* (perfect tense) amāvī = 'I have loved' and the *historic* (aorist or simple past) amāvī = 'I loved' which, of course, look identical. The perfect tense of a verb, although it refers to the past, is considered to be a *primary* tense because it describes the *present* result of an action occurring in the past. The aorist (or simple past) tense of a verb, by contrast, simply refers to an action which occurred in the past, with no reference to its present result.

E.g. librum lēgī = I have read the book.

E.g. librum herī lēgī = I read the book yesterday.

Exercise 7.6

Study the information above about the sequence of tenses. Translate into Latin:

1 He ran into the street to watch the animals.

2 I went to the city to see the temples of the Romans.

3 They were guarding the brave king lest he be captured by the enemy.

4 Hannibal led his forces across the mountains to overcome the Romans.

5 I sent the best slave to help you.

6 He had gone back to see his wretched father.

7 They came into the city lest they be killed by the enemy.

8 They hurried to the queen to praise her good works.

9 You were sailing to the island to see the inhabitants, weren't you?

10 You came to the fatherland to look at our temples, didn't you?

Irregular verbs in the subjunctive

The imperfect subjunctive of irregular verbs is easy, being formed in the normal way (by adding 'm', etc. to the present infinitive).

Imperfect subjunctive		
sum	**possum**	**ferō**
essem	possem	ferrem
essēs	possēs	ferrēs
esset	posset	ferret
essēmus	possēmus	ferrēmus
essētis	possētis	ferrētis
essent	possent	ferrent
eō	**volō**	**nōlō**
īrem	vellem	nōllem
īrēs	vellēs	nōllēs
īret	vellet	nōllet
īrēmus	vellēmus	nōllēmus
īrētis	vellētis	nōllētis
īrent	vellent	nōllent

The only one of these verbs to have a passive is ferō, which forms its imperfect subjunctive passive in an almost absurdly regular way:

ferrer, ferrēris, ferrētur, ferrēmur, ferrēminī, ferrentur.

Exercise 7.7

Translate into English:

1 Rōmānī nāvēs parāvērunt ut hostēs vincere possent.

2 senex ā mīlitibus interfectus est nē cibum ad cīvēs ferret.

3 mīlitēs captī sunt nē ad patriam redīrent.

4 nāvem dēlēvimus nē cōpiās ad hostēs ferret.

5 ad flūmen cucurrimus ut aquam invenīrēmus.

6 cīvēs in urbem ēgit ut tūtī essent.

7 in summum montem vēnī ut mare spectāre possem.

8 ad flūmen vēnī ut aquam in urbem ferrem.

9 ut terram dēfenderent mūrum maximum aedificāvērunt.

10 fēminae perterritae in urbem festīnāvērunt ut sē servārent.

Exercise 7.8

Read the following passage and answer the questions below.

The Romans take Spain, 206 B.C.

Rōmānī, quī plūrimās nāvēs habēbant, Poenōs in bellō semper superāre poterant. eī igitur, quod auxilium ā Graecīs petēbant, ad rēgem Macedoniae lēgātōs mīsērunt. hic tamen, nōmine Philippus, eōs iuvāre nōn poterat. deinde Rōmānī, quod bellum cōnficere cupiēbant, in Hispāniam festīnāvērunt. Publius Scīpiō
5 autem cum frātre Cnaeō suōs in illam terram dūxit ut Poenōs expelleret. hī autem ducēs in bellō interfectī sunt sed fīlius Publiī imperium mīlitum ā patribus Rōmānīs accēpit. hic, quī artī Hannibalis diū studuerat, peditēs circum aciem hostium mīsit, in medium agmen eōrum ruit. Poenōs autem quī cōpiās prope oppidum, nōmine Ilipam, īnstrūxerant paene dēlēvit. sīc Hispānia, ā Poenīs
10 āmissa, Rōmānīs trādita est.

Poenī, -ōrum, m. pl. = the Carthaginians	studeō, -ēre (+ dat.) = I study
lēgātus, -ī, m. = ambassador	pedes, -itis, m. = foot-soldier
cōnficiō, -ere = I complete	aciēs, aciēī, f. = battle line
Hispānia, -ae, f. = Spain	agmen, -inis, n. = column (of army)
expellō, -ere = I drive out	Ilipa, -ae, f. = Ilipa (a town in Spain)
imperium, -ī, n. = command	īnstruō, -ere, -ūxī = I draw up
patrēs: here = the Senators	āmittō, -ere, āmīsī, āmissum = I lose
ars, artis, f. = art, skill	

1 Rōmānī ... poterant (line 1). Why were the Romans able to overcome the Carthaginians?

2 eī igitur ... mīsērunt (lines 2–3). Why did the Carthaginians send ambassadors to the King of Macedonia?

3 hic ... poterat (line 3). How did the king react to the demands for help?

4 deinde ... festīnāvērunt (lines 3–4). Why did the Romans hurry into Spain?

5 Publius Scīpiō ... expelleret (lines 4–5). Why did the Scipio brothers lead their men into Spain?

6 hī ... interfectī sunt (lines 5–6). What happened to them when they got there?

7 sed fīlius ... accēpit (lines 6–7). To whom did the senate give command of the army?

8 hic ... ruit (lines 7–8). Describe the tactics used by the Roman general.

9 Poenōs ... dēlēvit (lines 8–9). How effective were these tactics?

10 plūrimās (line 1). What part of which adjective is this?

11 poterant (line 1). What part of which verb is this?

12 mīsērunt (line 3).

   (a) In which tense is this verb?

   (b) Give its principal parts.

13 frātre (line 5). In which case is this noun, and why?

14 expelleret (line 5). Explain why this verb is in the subjunctive.

15 quī (line 7). What sort of word is this? In which case is it?

16 trādita est (line 10). Explain the connection between this verb and the English word **tradition**.

Indirect command

You have already met direct commands and prohibitions, using the imperative for commands and nōlī/nōlīte + infinitive for prohibitions. **Indirect** commands are introduced by verbs of ordering, warning, begging, advising, forbidding, etc., and are generally expressed using ut + the subjunctive (for commands) or nē + the subjunctive (for prohibitions). As with final clauses, the sequence of tenses applies.

E.g. eum monuit ut venīret = He advised him to come.
      eum rogāvit nē venīret = He asked him not to come.

Verbs taking this construction include: rogō = I ask; moneō = I advise; imperō (+ dat.) = I order; persuādeō (+ dat.) = I persuade; petō = I seek (in the sense of 'I ask' or 'I beg').

E.g. mihi persuāsit ut venīrem = He persuaded me to come (lit. = he persuaded me that I might come).

E.g. cōpiās suās monuit ut oppidum oppugnārent = He advised his forces to attack the town (lit. = he encouraged his forces that they might attack the town).

E.g. ā mē petīvit ut venīrem = He asked me to come (lit. = he sought from me that I might come).

Exercise 7.9

Translate into English:

1 dux Rōmānīs imperāvit ut cum hostibus pugnārent.

2 prīnceps cōpiīs imperāvit ut oppidum oppugnārent.

3 amīcō meō persuāsī ut mātrem meam salūtāret.

4 nōs monuērunt ut equum caperēmus.

5 dux suīs persuāsit nē sagittās relinquerent.

6 magister puerōs parvōs monuit ut ancillam vocārent.

7 rēx ā custōde petēbat ut cīvēs occīderet.

8 cīvēs rēgem monuērunt ut pugnāret.

9 agricola fīlium rogāvit ut equōs in agrum dūceret.

10 hic mīles cīvēs rogāvit nē in montēs fugerent.

Exercise 7.10

Study the information above about indirect commands. Then translate into Latin:

1 He ordered (using imperō) the slave to hurry.

2 He ordered (using imperō) the soldiers to fight.

3 They advised us not to come to the city.

4 They ordered us (using imperō) to fight.

5 The slave advised his master to punish the boys.

6 The leader ordered (using imperō) his forces to build a wall.

7 The enemy advised us to flee.

8 He advised me to remain.

9 Why were we asked (using rogō) to fight?

10 Who ordered you (using imperō) to return to the city, girls?

Verbs followed by an infinitive

You have now learnt how to cope with indirect commands using ut/nē (+ subjunctive).

But *some* verbs of ordering and the like take a simple infinitive (as in English). These are:

    iubeō = I order; volō = I want; nōlō = I do not want;
    cōgō = I force; cupiō = I desire.

E.g. He ordered me to come = mē iussit venīre.

This construction is obviously very much easier than the other one. However, the complication is that you now have to learn which verb takes which construction.

N.B. It is worth pointing out that, when in English we say 'tell', we often mean 'order'.

E.g. He *told* him to do it (i.e. He *ordered* him to do it) = eum iussit id facere.

Exercise 7.11

Study the information above about indirect commands. Notice how some verbs take the ut/nē (+ the subjunctive) construction, and some take a simple infinitive.

Now translate into Latin:

1 They ordered me to come to Rome (using iubeō).

2 He did not want me to come to Rome (using nōlō).

3 He wanted me to remain in the town (using volō).

4 They wanted me to fight with the enemy (using cupiō).

5 The king forced him to flee (using cōgō).

Exercise 7.12

Translate into English:

1 dux imperāvit mīlitibus ut arma in eō locō parārent.

2 mulier iuvenēs iussit librum legere.

3 cīvēs Rōmānī mē monuērunt nē id facerem.

4 puellam iussimus in templum currere.

5 pater nōluit puerōs vīnum bibere.

Exercise 7.13

Read the following passage and answer the questions below.

Hercules completes his labours

postquam <u>aurea</u> <u>māla</u> ad Eurystheum <u>relāta</u> sunt, hic <u>Herculī</u> imperāvit ut <u>canem</u>
Cerberum ex <u>Orcō</u> in lūcem ferret. hic labōrum omnium difficillimus erat. nēmō
enim <u>umquam</u> ex <u>Orcō</u> vīvus redierat. Cerberus autem, cui tria capita erant,
<u>sēdem</u> <u>Plūtōnis</u>, rēgis <u>Orcī</u>, custōdiēbat. Herculēs igitur ad <u>rīpam</u> flūminis <u>Stygis</u>
5 iter fēcit. ibi <u>Charontem</u> cōnspexit, quī <u>mānēs</u> trāns flūmen in <u>cumbā</u> <u>trānsportābat</u>.
huic Herculēs imperāvit ut trāns flūmen sē <u>trānsportāret</u> sed, propter <u>pondus</u>
maximum virī fortis, nōluit. tandem tamen, ab Hercule coāctus, Charōn <u>cumbam</u>
trāns flūmen tūtam <u>rēmigāvit</u>.
inde Herculēs ad <u>sēdem</u> ipsam Plūtōnis <u>pervēnit</u>. hīc <u>canis</u> saevus rēgem
10 rēgīnamque eius custōdiēbat. Herculēs tamen nōn timēbat et rēgem <u>ōrāvit</u> ut
<u>canem</u> illum sibi daret. 'iussus sum <u>canem</u> tuum ex <u>Orcō</u> in lūcem ferre,' inquit.
'nōnne mē iuvābis?' Plūtō Herculem <u>benignē</u> accēpit et eum iuvāre volēbat.
Cerberum tamen magnopere amābat. eī igitur imperāvit ut labōrem <u>cōnficeret</u>
sed <u>canem</u> ad sē posteā <u>redūceret</u>. sīc Herculēs <u>canem</u> illum ex <u>Orcō</u> trāxit et ad
15 Eurystheum dūxit. ille perterritus est et Herculem <u>ōrāvit</u>, multīs cum <u>lacrimīs</u>, ut
<u>canem</u> occīderet aut in <u>Orcum</u> <u>redūceret</u>. hic labor omnium quōs Eurystheus eī
dederat <u>ultimus</u> erat. duodecim labōrēs <u>cōnfectī</u> sunt et <u>servitūte</u>, magnō cum
gaudiō, Herculēs tandem līberātus est.

aureus, -a, -um = golden	cumba, -ae, f. = small boat
mālum, -ī, n. = apple	trānsportō, -āre = I carry across
referō, referre = I carry back	pondus, -eris, n. = weight
Herculēs, -is, m. = Hercules	rēmigō, -āre = I row
canis, canis, m. = dog	perveniō, -īre = I reach
Orcus, -ī, m. = the Underworld	ōrō, -āre = I beg
umquam = ever	benignē = kindly
sēdēs, -is, f. = seat, abode	cōnficiō, -ere, -fēcī, -fectum = I complete
Plūtō, -ōnis, m. = Pluto	redūcō, -ere = I lead back
rīpa, -ae, f. = bank	trahō, -ere, trāxī = I drag
Styx, Stygis, f. = Styx (the river of the Underworld)	lacrima, -ae, f. = tear
	ultimus, -a, -um = last
Charōn, -ontis, m. = Charon (the ferry man)	servitūs, -ūtis, f. = slavery
mānēs, -ium, m. pl. = the spirits of the dead	gaudium, -ī, n. = joy

1 hic Herculī ... ferret (lines 1–2). What did Eurystheus command Hercules to do?

2 hic labor ... redierat (lines 2–3). How is this task described, and why?

3 Cerberus ... custōdiēbat (lines 3–4). How is Cerberus described in these lines?

4 ibi Charontem ... trānsportābat (line 5). Whom did Hercules see on the banks of the River Styx and what did this person do?

5 huic ... trānsportāret (line 6). What did Hercules do when he met Charon?

6 sed ... nōluit (lines 6–7). How did Charon respond, and why?

7 From the second paragraph (lines 9–18), give in Latin one example of each of the following:

   (a) a preposition followed by the ablative case

   (b) a perfect passive participle

   (c) a verb in the subjunctive

   (d) a 3rd declension adjective

   (e) a demonstrative pronoun in the dative case.

8 ipsam (line 9). In which case and gender is this word? Give its nominative singular masculine form.

9 labōrēs (line 17). Explain the connection between this word and the English word **laborious**.

10 līberātus est (line 18). In which tense and voice is this verb?

11 Translate into Latin:

   (a) He was setting free all the slaves.

   (b) The terrified women ran into the city.

12 Translate the second paragraph into English.

Vocabulary 7

Latin	English
Verbs	
imperō, -āre, -āvī, -ātum (+ dat.)	I order
persuādeō, -ēre, persuāsī, persuāsum (+ dat.)	I persuade
Conjunctions	
aut	or
nē	lest, in order that ... not
ut (+ subjunctive)	in order to

Death and burial

The Romans believed that it was very important to observe the proper rites of burial when someone died, otherwise their soul would never find rest. The most important part of these rites was to scatter three handfuls of dust over the corpse and put a small coin, an obol, in the dead person's mouth. This coin was used to pay Charon, the ferryman, to row the dead body over the River Styx and into the Underworld. When they had crossed the River Styx, the souls of the dead (mānēs) drank the water of the River Lethe, which caused them to forget everything about their mortal lives. They then came to the abode of Pluto himself, the King of the Underworld, where they faced judgement by three judges, Minos, Rhadamanthus and Aeacus. The good were led into the Elysian Fields, a place of paradise; the bad were led into Tartarus where they faced eternal punishment.

> This topic is part of the Non-Linguistic Studies section of the ISEB syllabus.

Exercise 7.14

(a) (i) Tell the story of Hercules's adventure in the Underworld.

   (ii) Which of his twelve labours do you think was the most difficult, and why?

(b) (i) Outline the Romans' approach to death and burial.

   (ii) What differences and similarities are there between the Roman and our own attitudes to death?

Roman tombstones

Much can be learnt about the Romans from the tombstones that have survived. These typically give information about the dead person and their family, and if the tombstone is from a military grave, it tells us about where and with whom the soldier served.

> This topic is part of the Non-Linguistic Studies section of the ISEB syllabus.

■ Charon receiving a dead person's soul, depicted on a lekythos (a pot used to store oil) from Ancient Greece

A typical tombstone will begin with the abbreviation D.M., short for Dīs Mānibus (to the gods of the Underworld), and then list the dead person's praenōmen (first name), nōmen (clan name) and cognōmen (family name). The praenomen was often abbreviated, as follows:

A. = Aulus	M. = Marcus	Sp. = Spurius
C. = Gāius	P. = Publius	T. = Titus
Cn. = Gnaeus	Q. = Quintus	Ti. = Tiberius
D. = Decimus	S. = Sextus	
L. = Lūcius	Ser. = Servius	

Further details of the information that can be found on tombstones is available in *Greeks & Romans* by A. M. Wright, published by Galore Park.

8 4th declension; deponent verbs

4th declension nouns

Most 4th declension nouns decline like gradus and they are almost all masculine.

gradus, -ūs, m. = step	Singular	Plural
Nominative	grad-us	grad-ūs
Vocative	grad-us	grad-ūs
Accusative	grad-um	grad-ūs
Genitive	grad-ūs	grad-uum
Dative	grad-uī	grad-ibus
Ablative	grad-ū	grad-ibus

Points to note

1 4th declension nouns are a bit of a nightmare, because they look like 2nd declension nouns in the nominative singular, but then go completely pear-shaped. You can tell that they are 4th declension by the genitive singular in -ūs (rhyming with *juice*).

2 Extreme care needs to be taken when translating Latin which contains 4th declension nouns, owing to the fact that the -us ending of the nominative and vocative singular can easily be confused with the -ūs ending, which occurs no less than four times.

3 All the 4th declension nouns in -us that you meet in this book are masculine except manus = hand and domus = house, which are feminine.

Irregular 4th declension noun: domus

The Latin for a 'house' or 'home' is irregular, taking its endings from the 2nd and 4th declensions almost at random. Rarer forms are given in brackets.

domus, domūs, f. = house		
	Singular	Plural
Nominative	dom-us	dom-ūs
Vocative	dom-us	dom-ūs
Accusative	dom-um	dom-ōs (dom-ūs)
Genitive	dom-ūs	dom-uum (dom-ōrum)
Dative	dom-uī (dom-ō)	dom-ibus
Ablative	dom-ō	dom-ibus

Note that, as with towns and small islands, when going *to* or *from* domus, no preposition is used. Note also that the locative case of domus is domī (= at home).

E.g.   mulierēs domum festīnāvērunt = The women hurried home.
mulierēs domī habitābant = The women lived at home.

Exercise 8.1

Study the information above about 4th declension nouns. Note the way that 2nd and 4th declension nouns can be distinguished by looking at their genitive singular: 2nd declension nouns go -ī, 4th declension nouns go -ūs. Then decline in full:

1   manus, manūs, f. = hand

2   exercitus, exercitūs, m. = army

3   portus, portūs, m. = harbour

4   oculus, oculī, m. = eye

Exercise 8.2

Translate into Latin:

1   He will lead the army towards the harbour.

2   The leader of the army was a brave soldier.

3   The enemy were defending the homes of the inhabitants.

4   All the old men were sitting near the harbour.

5   Yesterday my father wounded the good slave's hand.

6   He looked at the walls of the house.

7   The king advised the chief to lead his army home.

8   We will lead the armies towards the river.

9   We were sitting on the steps of the beautiful house.

10   The farmer carried the food in his large hands.

Exercise 8.3

Translate into English:

1 dominus servī domum novam eī dedit.

2 nostrī in gradibus templī tēlīs et gladiīs pugnābant.

3 dux exercitūs mīlitēs in montēs dūxit.

4 nautās miserōs in portū hostium tenēbāmus.

5 omnēs servī ex domō veniēbant ut ad portum currerent.

6 vōs in montibus ambulāre aut in flumine lūdere cupitis.

7 num domōs prope portum aedificābitis?

8 nōnne ducī exercitūs ut urbem oppugnāret imperāvit?

9 nōs tūtī in portum multīs cum nāvibus nāvigāvimus.

10 quis pecūniam rēgis in manibus fert?

Go further

The future perfect tense

There is one more tense in Latin to learn, the future perfect. It is used to describe what you *will have* done, and goes as follows:

Active	Passive
amāverō	amātus erō
amāveris	amātus eris
amāverit	amātus erit
amāverimus	amātī erimus
amāveritis	amātī eritis
amāverint	amātī erunt

It is not a very common tense, but it is nice to have learnt all the indicative tenses, rather than having one lurking unlearnt at the back of the book.

Deponent verbs

A deponent verb is *passive in form* but *active in meaning*. That is, it looks passive but should be translated as if it were active. E.g. cōnātur = he is trying; cōnātus sum = I have tried.

A deponent verb has only three principal parts. These can be compared to the passive of the regular verb as follows:

cōnor   **cōnārī**   **cōnātus sum**
I try   to try   I have tried

amor	amārī	amātus sum
I am loved	to be loved	I have been loved

You can tell to which conjugation a deponent verb belongs by studying its principal parts and comparing these to the passive of the regular conjugations. We will start with 1st conjugation verbs.

Deponent verbs of the 1st conjugation

1st conjugation deponent verbs have principal parts in -or, -ārī, -ātus sum:

cōnor, cōnārī, cōnātus sum = I try	
Present	**Perfect**
cōn-or	cōnāt-us sum
cōnā-ris	cōnāt-us es
cōnā-tur	cōnāt-us est
cōnā-mur	cōnāt-ī sumus
cōnā-minī	cōnāt-ī estis
cōna-ntur	cōnāt-ī sunt
Future	**Future perfect**
cōnā-bor	cōnāt-us erō
cōnā-beris	cōnāt-us eris
cōnā-bitur	cōnāt-us erit
cōnā-bimur	cōnāt-ī erimus
cōnā-biminī	cōnāt-ī eritis
cōnā-buntur	cōnāt-ī erunt
Imperfect	**Pluperfect**
cōnā-bar	cōnāt-us eram
cōnā-bāris	cōnāt-us erās
cōnā-bātur	cōnāt-us erat
cōnā-bāmur	cōnāt-ī erāmus
cōnā-bāminī	cōnāt-ī erātis
cōnā-bantur	cōnāt-ī erant

As you would expect, the -us in the perfect stem tenses has to agree with the subject:

E.g. The girl has tried = puella cōnāta est.

Exercise 8.4

Study the information above about deponent verbs. You must be familiar with the *passive infinitives* of regular verbs if you are to be able to recognise the conjugation of a deponent verb. Note that the tenses of a deponent verb are identical to the *passive* tenses of verbs of that conjugation. Now write out the following tenses:

1 amō in the present *passive*

2 mīror, mīrārī, mīrātus sum = 'I wonder at' in the present tense

3 amō in the future *passive*

4 hortor, hortārī, hortātus sum = 'I encourage' in the future tense

5 amō in the imperfect *passive*

6 moror, morārī, morātus sum = 'I delay' in the imperfect tense

7 Perfect *passive* of amō

8 Perfect tense of hortor

9 Pluperfect *passive* of amō

10 Pluperfect tense of hortor

Exercise 8.5

Translate into Latin:

1 He is encouraging the proud farmers.

2 We were trying to watch the boy.

3 They were trying to find the wine.

4 I will encourage my soldiers.

5 She encouraged many citizens.

6 You (sing.) were trying to encourage me for many hours.

7 On the fifth day he will encourage his daughter.

8 The angry women have encouraged the boy.

9 The soldiers have tried to overcome the enemy.

10 The wise sailor had tried to depart because of the storm.

Deponent verbs of the 2nd conjugation

2nd conjugation verbs have principal parts in -eor, -ērī and go like
the passive of moneō.

videor, vidērī, vīsus sum = I seem	
Present	Perfect
vide-or	vīs-us sum
vidē-ris	vīs-us es
vidē-tur	vīs-us est
vidē-mur	vīs-ī sumus
vidē-minī	vīs-ī estis
vide-ntur	vīs-ī sunt

Future	Future perfect
vidē-bor	vīs-us erō
vidē-beris	vīs-us eris
vidē-bitur	vīs-us erit
vidē-bimur	vīs-ī erimus
vidē-biminī	vīs-ī eritis
vidē-buntur	vīs-ī erunt
Imperfect	**Pluperfect**
vidē-bar	vīs-us eram
vidē-bāris	vīs-us erās
vidē-bātur	vīs-us erat
vidē-bāmur	vīs-ī erāmus
vidē-bāminī	vīs-ī erātis
vidē-bantur	vīs-ī erant

Note that videor can be used as the passive of videō to mean I am seen, or as a deponent verb meaning I seem.

Deponent verbs of the 3rd, 4th and mixed conjugations

Examples of 3rd, 4th and mixed conjugation deponent verbs are shown below:

> 3rd: loquor, loquī, locūtus sum = I speak
> 4th: partior, partīrī, partītus sum = I share
> Mixed: morior, morī, mortuus sum = I die

Present		
loqu-or = I speak	parti-or = I share	mori-or = I die
loqu-eris	partī-ris	mor-eris
loqu-itur	partī-tur	mor-itur
loqu-imur	partī-mur	mor-imur
loqu-iminī	partī-minī	mor-iminī
loqu-untur	parti-untur	mori-untur
Future		
loqu-ar	parti-ar	mori-ar
loqu-ēris	parti-ēris	mori-ēris
loqu-ētur	parti-ētur	mori-ētur
loqu-ēmur	parti-ēmur	mori-ēmur
loqu-ēminī	parti-ēminī	mori-ēminī
loqu-entur	parti-entur	mori-entur

Imperfect		
loqu-ēbar	parti-ēbar	mori-ēbar
loqu-ēbāris	parti-ēbāris	mori-ēbāris
loqu-ēbātur	parti-ēbātur	mori-ēbātur
loqu-ēbāmur	parti-ēbāmur	mori-ēbāmur
loqu-ēbāminī	parti-ēbāminī	mori-ēbāminī
loqu-ēbantur	parti-ēbantur	mori-ēbantur

Exercise 8.6

Read the information above about deponent verbs. Now translate into English:

1 Rōmānī urbem parvam oppugnāre nōn cōnābuntur.

2 iuvenēs multīs cum amicīs in montēs profectī sunt.

3 puellae miserae propter bellum diū passae erant.

4 omnēs de animālibus saevīs loquī volēbant.

5 poēta superbus propter opera sua laudātus est.

6 postquam nūntiī profectī sunt paucī incolae discessērunt.

7 mulierēs cum līberīs parvīs in agrōs prōgrediēbantur.

8 quis ducem alium in proelium sequī vult?

9 mīlitēs fortēs prō patriā morī volēbant.

10 nōnne haec verba sapientissima senex locūtus est?

Exercise 8.7

Translate into Latin:

1 He seems to be happy.

2 She has been seen in the street.

3 They went out of the city.

4 They went into the city.

5 She has spoken to her mother.

6 In war soldiers will always die.

7 The enemy set out to cross the mountains.

8 We set out on the third day.

9 We advanced but at last were defeated by the enemy.

10 You (pl.) will follow the leader of the army into the mountains.

Exercise 8.8

Revision of verb forms. Translate into English:

1 monent.

2 monentur.

3 regent.

4 regentur.

5 audiēmus.

6 audiēmur.

7 cēpit.

8 capit.

9 capiet.

10 vident.

11 vidēminī.

12 vīsum est.

13 vīsa est.

14 amārī.

15 cōgere.

16 cōgī.

17 capī.

18 fuī.

19 esse.

20 interficiēris.

Deponent verbs in the subjunctive

When forming the imperfect subjunctive of a *deponent* verb, you need to establish which conjugation the verb is and then follow the pattern of that verb type in the passive.

E.g. loquor, loquī, locūtus sum follows regō. regō in the imperfect subjunctive passive goes regerer, regerēris, regerētur; thus loquor goes loquerer, loquerēris, loquerētur, etc.

Intransitive verbs in the passive

As you know, intransitive verbs are verbs which cannot govern a direct object (e.g. I walk, I swim, etc.). Note that some verbs which are transitive in English are intransitive in Latin, e.g. pugnō = 'I fight' (in Latin, one never 'fights someone', one 'fights *with* someone'). An intransitive verb can only be used in the passive *impersonally* (i.e. the subject of the verb is the word 'it').

E.g. pugnātum est = it was fought, i.e. there was fighting.

N.B. this also applies to verbs which take the dative, e.g. persuādeō.

E.g. I persuade you = tibi persuādeō; but
I am persuaded by you = mihi persuādētur ā tē (i.e. it is persuaded to me by you).

Exercise 8.9

Read the following passage and answer the questions below.

Jason sets out in search of the golden fleece

erant ōlim duo frātrēs, Aesōn et Peliās. eōrum Aesōn <u>nātū maior</u> erat et, ubi
pater mortuus est, <u>rēgnum</u> <u>obtinuit</u>. Peliās tamen, quod magnopere regere
cupiēbat, rēgnum <u>rapuit</u>, frātrem <u>expulit</u>, fīlium frātris interficere cōnātus est.
fīlius ille, nōmine Iāsōn, dē perīculō monitus, in <u>aliēnam</u> terram profectus est.
5 <u>brevī</u> <u>tempore</u> posteā, Peliās amīcum <u>Delphōs</u> mīsit ut <u>ōrāculum</u> <u>cōnsuleret</u>.
<u>Pythia</u> autem rēgem monuit ut <u>cavēret</u> <u>peregrīnum</u> ūnum <u>calceum</u> gerentem.
multōs annōs Iasōn <u>apud</u> <u>Centaurum</u> <u>quendam</u> habitābat sed tandem in patriam
suam <u>regrēssus</u> est. ille iuvenis flūmen trānsiēns alterum <u>calceum</u> forte <u>āmīsit</u>.
ubi igitur illum <u>peregrīnum</u> unum <u>modǒ</u> <u>calceum</u> gerentem cōnspexit, rēx Peliās
10 perterritus Iāsōnī ut <u>vellus</u> <u>aureum</u> peteret imperāvit. hoc autem opus difficillimum
esse crēdidit. <u>vellus</u> enim rēx <u>quīdam</u>, nōmine Aeētēs, in <u>Colchide</u> rēgnō suō
<u>dīligenter</u> custōdiēbat.
Iāson multōs comitēs lēgit, inter quōs erant Herculēs, Thēseus, Orpheus, Castor,
et in nāve nōtissimā, cui nōmen erat Argō, profectus est. virī hī fortissimī multa
15 perīcula superāvērunt, <u>Harpyiās</u> <u>dispulērunt</u>, <u>Symplēgadas</u> <u>ēvāsērunt</u>. tandem ad
terram Colchida advēnērunt.

nātū maior = older	Centaurus, -ī, m. = Centaur (half-man, half-horse)
rēgnum, -ī, n. = kingdom	
obtineō, -ēre = I hold	quīdam = a certain
rapiō, -ere, rapuī, raptum = I seize	regredior, -ī, regressus sum = I go back
expellō, -ere, expulī = I drive out	āmittō, -ere = I lose
aliēnus, -a, -um = foreign	modǒ = only
brevis, -e = short	vellus, -eris, n. = fleece
tempus, -oris, n. = time	aureus, -a, -um = golden
Delphī, -ōrum, m. pl. = Delphi	Colchis, -idis, f. = Colchis
ōrāculum, -ī, n. = the oracle	dīligenter = carefully
cōnsulō, -ere = I consult	Harpyiae, -ārum, f. pl. = the Harpies (birds with the heads of women)
Pythia, -ae, f. = the Pythia (a priestess at Delphi)	
	dispellō, -ere, -pulī, -pulsum = I drive off
caveō, -ēre = I beware	
peregrīnus, -ī, m. = stranger	Symplēgades, -um, f. pl. = the Symplegades (clashing rocks)
calceus, -ī, m. = shoe	
apud (+ acc.) = at the house of	ēvādō, -ere = I avoid

1 erant … obtinuit (lines 1–2). What are we told about Aeson and Pelias in these lines?

2 Peliās tamen … cōnātus est (lines 2–3). What did Pelias do when his father died and why?

3 fīlius ille … profectus est (line 4). How did Jason react to events?

4 brevī … cōnsuleret (line 5). What did Pelias ask a friend to do?

5 Pythia … gerentem (line 6). What advice did the king receive from the Pythia?

6 Translate the second paragraph (lines 7–12).

7 From the third paragraph, give one example of:

   (a) a deponent verb

   (b) a superlative adjective

   (c) a relative pronoun.

8 comitēs (line 13). Which case of which noun is this?

9 quōs (line 13). To which noun does this refer?

10 nāve (line 14). In which case is this noun and why?

11 multa (line 14). Give the comparative and superlative (nom. sing. masc.) of this adjective.

12 hī (line 14). What type of word is this? Give its nominative singular masculine.

13 superāvērunt (line 15). This verb means **they overcame**. How would you say in Latin **they will overcome**?

14 advēnērunt (line 16). Explain the connection between this word and the English word **advent**.

■ Jason captures the Golden Fleece with help from Medea, depicted on a Roman sarcophagus

Vocabulary 8

Latin	English
Nouns	
domus, -ūs, f.	house
exercitus, -ūs, m.	army
manus, -ūs, f.	hand
portus, -ūs, m.	harbour
Verbs	
conor, -ārī, conātus sum	I try
ēgredior, ēgredī, ēgressus sum	I go out
hortor, -ārī, hortātus sum	I encourage, urge
ingredior, ingredī, ingressus sum	I go in, enter
loquor, loquī, locūtus sum	I speak
morior, morī, mortuus sum	I die
patior, patī, passus sum	I suffer, allow
proficīscor, proficīscī, profectus sum	I set out
prōgredior, prōgredī, prōgressus sum	I advance
sequor, sequī, secūtus sum	I follow

9 Ablative absolute; indirect statement

◯ The ablative absolute

An ablative absolute consists of a noun or pronoun in the ablative, together with a participle agreeing with it. Ablative absolutes are often used in Latin to state the circumstances under which an action takes place. They may thus be said to be 'setting the scene' for the rest of the sentence.

An ablative absolute may be used with any type of participle, as follows:

1 Present participle

E.g. **puellā spectante**, pater discessit = **(With) the girl watching**, the father departed.

The noun puellā is in the ablative (thus 'with the girl') and the participle spectante agrees with it (thus 'watching'). This can be put into more natural English as follows: 'While the girl was watching, the father departed.'

N.B. A present participle has its ablative singular ending in -e (rather than -ī) when used in an ablative absolute.

2 Perfect participle passive

E.g. **puellā monitā**, pater discessit = **(With) the girl having been warned**, the father departed; or: After the girl had been warned, the father departed.

3 Perfect participle deponent

With deponent verbs, the perfect participle is, of course, active in meaning, allowing us to say things such as 'having followed' or 'having set out'.

E.g. **puellā profectā**, pater discessit = **(With) the girl having set out**, the father departed; or: After the girl had set out, the father departed.

A word of advice

The best way to cope with ablative absolutes is to translate them literally first, i.e. using a phrase such as 'with the girl having been loved'. Only then should you try to put it into real English. It is, of course, essential that you identify the *tense* of the participle correctly (i.e. is it 'loving' or 'having been loved'?). You should be particularly careful not to confuse the perfect participle passive of a normal transitive verb with the perfect participle of a *deponent* verb. *Only deponent verbs can have a perfect participle with an active meaning.*

E.g.   secūtus = having followed;

profectus = having set out; *but*

monitus = having *been* warned.

Exercise 9.1

Study the information above about ablative absolutes. Then translate the following into English:

1 hostibus victīs ...

2 patre spectante ...

3 agricolā monitō ...

4 rēgīnā regente ...

5 librīs lēctīs ...

6 servō discēdente ...

7 aquā parātā ...

8 tēlīs iactīs ...

9 nūntiīs missīs ...

10 exercitū profectō ...

Exercise 9.2

Translate the following phrases into Latin, using the ablative absolute construction:

1 After the king had been killed ...

2 After these things had been done ...

3 When the woman had been warned ...

4 While the young man was following ...

5 While the girls were fleeing ...

Exercise 9.3

Translate into English:

1 hostibus vīsīs, dux exercitum suum in oppidum celeriter dūxit.

2 armīs prope flūmen positīs, Rōmānī ad cīvēs prōgressī sunt.

3 librīs ā puerīs lēctīs, magister patrī eōrum loquēbātur.

4 poētā sīc locūtō, cīvēs magnopere timēbant.

5 verbīs iuvenis audītīs, servus līberātus est.

6 animālī ā mīlite occīsō, omnēs cīvēs egressī sunt.

7 ancillae, cibō parātō, domum ingressae sunt.

8 urbe ab hostibus captā, mīlitēs profectī sunt.

9 nāvibus tempestāte dēlētīs, nautae in portum prōgressī sunt.

10 nōnne mūrō aedificātō urbs tūtissima erit?

Exercise 9.4

Translate into Latin, using ablative absolutes where appropriate:

1 After the slaves had been warned, the master returned home.

2 While the wife was watching, the man punished his children.

3 When the soldier had been killed, the citizens went back to the city.

4 After the Romans had set out, the inhabitants fled towards the mountains.

5 When the ships were destroyed, all the sailors were very sad.

6 After the town had been attacked by the enemy, the citizens departed.

7 While the boys were singing, the men were working well at home.

8 After the queen had been praised, the king gave many gifts to the citizens.

9 Once the horse had been captured, the farmer hurried into the town.

10 Once the swords and spears had been collected, the chief gave a reward to his men.

More on ablative absolutes

1 An ablative absolute is often used to translate an English temporal or causal clause (referring to time and cause respectively). Very often these will have to be 'turned' to allow the passive participle to be used. This is because, unless we are using a deponent verb, there is no way in Latin of saying 'having loved', or 'having prepared', so instead we have to turn it round and say 'having been loved', 'having been prepared', etc.
E.g. After she had prepared the gifts, she returned home
(i.e. (With) the gifts having been prepared, she returned home)
= dōnīs parātīs, domum rediit.

2 An ablative absolute must *not* be used to refer to any noun or pronoun grammatically connected in any way to the verb in the

main clause. For example, a noun cannot be put into an ablative absolute if it goes on to be the subject or object of the main clause.

E.g. After the boy had been seen, he (i.e. the boy) went home = puer vīsus domum rediit.

An ablative absolute could not have been used for the 'boy had been seen', because the boy went on to be the *subject* of the verb in the main clause. Instead, the boy is in the nominative and vīsus agrees with him; and thus the whole thing means 'the having been seen boy returned home'.

E.g. After the soldiers had been captured, the king killed them (i.e. the soldiers) = rēx mīlitēs captōs interfēcit.

An ablative absolute could not have been used for 'the soldiers had been captured', because they went on to be the *object* of the verb in the main clause. Instead we write 'the king killed the having been captured soldiers'.

Exercise 9.5

Study the further information above about ablative absolutes. Then translate into English:

1 templīs ā prīncipe aedificātīs, cīvēs cibum nōn habēbant.

2 templa ā prīncipe aedificāta laudābant.

3 omnēs mīlitēs in proeliō captī interfectī sunt.

4 gladium celeriter captum in corpus servī pepulit.

5 puellā cōnspectā, magister puerum domum redūxit.

6 īnsulā subitō vīsā, nautae iterum laetī erant.

7 cōpiās trāns montēs ductās Rōmānī spectābant.

8 cōpiīs trāns montēs ductīs, dux in Ītaliam festīnāre cupiēbat.

9 cōpiae trāns montēs ductae ducem in Ītaliam sequēbantur.

10 urbe ab hostibus frūstrā oppugnātā, prope flūmen trēs hōrās pugnātum est.

Exercise 9.6

Translate into Latin, being sure not to use an ablative absolute if it involves a noun or pronoun grammatically connected to the verb in the main clause:

1 After the Romans had captured the women, they killed them.

2 While the sailors were looking for water, the soldiers advanced.

3 While the king was watching, the whole army set out.

4 After throwing their spears, the soldiers fled.

5 Because their ships had been destroyed by the storm, the sailors decided to remain in the harbour.

6 While the farmer was preparing the wine, we were talking in the street.

Exercise 9.7

Translate into English:

1 cīvēs sapientēs in viā stantēs deōs laudābant.

2 nostrīs ā Graecīs superātīs, cīvēs auxilium petīvērunt.

3 incolīs ad mare pulsīs, Rōmānī templa maxima dēlēre cōnātī sunt.

4 tempestāte magnā pulsī, nautae terram frūstrā petēbant.

5 fēminīs sequentibus, virī septem in agrōs regressī sunt.

Exercise 9.8

Translate into English:

Saved by the oxen, 217 BC

hīs <u>victōriīs partīs</u>, Hannibal Rōmam ipsam prōgredī cupiēbat. <u>Poenī</u> tamen, incolīs <u>nūllō</u> <u>modō</u> iuvantibus, urbem sine plūribus cōpiīs capere nōn poterant. trāns Ītaliam, igitur, Rōmānīs sequentibus, Hannibal exercitum suum dūcēbat.

dux Rōmānus, nōmine Q. Fabius Maximus, hostēs diū spectābat nec tamen
5 cum eīs pugnābat. hostēs tamen paene cēpit ubī eōs in <u>saltum</u> quī inter montēs <u>quōsdam</u> <u>ferēbat</u> pepulit. Rōmānī <u>castra</u> circum <u>Poenōs</u> posuerant neque hī fugere poterant. Poenī, tamen, plūrimōs <u>bovēs</u> cēperant, quōrum <u>cornua</u> multīs <u>virgīs decorāverant</u>. hōs, virgīs <u>incēnsīs</u>, ad Rōmānōs pepulērunt. Rōmānī, aliī <u>mīrātī</u>, aliī territī, <u>aciem</u> relīquērunt et Poenī <u>effugere</u> poterant.

---

victoriam pariō, -ere, peperī, partum = I win a victory
Poenī, -ōrum, m. pl. = Carthaginians
nūllus, -a, -um = no
modus, -ī, m. = way
saltus, -ūs, m. = pass
quīdam = certain
ferō: here = I lead
castra, -ōrum, n. pl. = camp
bōs, bovis, c. = ox or cow
cornū, -ūs, n. = horn
virga, -ae, f. = twig
decorō, -āre = I decorate, adorn
incendō, -ere, incendī, incēnsum = I set fire to
mīror, -ārī, mīrātus sum = I wonder at
aciēs, -ēī, f. = battle line
effugiō, -ere = I escape

◯ Indirect statement

After verbs of saying, knowing, believing, perceiving, hearing and other similar verbs, we often have an indirect statement; that is, the words of the speaker are reported *indirectly*.

E.g. He says that the Romans are attacking the town.

In Latin, indirect statement follows the **accusative and infinitive** construction, whereby the subject of the indirect statement is put in the accusative and the verb is put in the infinitive. The object, if there is one, remains unchanged in the accusative.

E.g. dīcō **servum labōrāre** = I say that the slave is working (literally: I say the slave to work, i.e. to be working).

E.g. dīcit **Rōmānōs** oppidum **oppugnāre** = He says that the Romans are attacking the town (literally: he says the Romans to attack the town, i.e. to be attacking the town).

This is one of the most common constructions used in Latin, so make sure you master it!

◯ Active tenses of the infinitive

So far you have met only the present infinitive, active and passive. But in fact, infinitives in Latin exist in the future and perfect as well. This is very lucky, actually, because, apart from the fact that it is nice to have some more grammar to learn, we *need* these different tenses to cope with the different types of indirect statement. Here are the three active infinitives:

1 **Present**
   You already know these:
   amāre, monēre, regere, audīre, capere (to love, to warn, etc.)

2 **Future**
   These are formed from the supine, by changing -um to -ūrus esse. In other words, they are the future participle of the verb, with esse (= to be) added on the end to make it an infinitive.
   E.g. amātūrus esse, monitūrus esse, etc. (to be about to love, to be about to warn, etc.)
   The -us bit of the participle declines like bonus, as you would expect.
   N.B. The future infinitive, although not on the CASE syllabus, is a very useful form to learn, and incredibly easy to recognise. Think about the word FUT**UR**E, and notice how future infinitives contain the letters -ur- and you should have no difficulty with these.

3 **Perfect**
   These are formed from the perfect stem, by adding -isse.
   E.g. amāvisse, monuisse, rēxisse, etc. (to have loved, to have warned, etc.)

Using these three active infinitives, we can write three different types of indirect statement:

Present: He says that the enemy **are coming** = dīcit hostēs **venīre.**
Future: He says that the enemy **will come** = dīcit hostēs **ventūrōs esse.**
Perfect: He says that the enemy **have come** = dīcit hostēs **vēnisse.**

Exercise 9.9

Study the information above about indirect statements. Then translate into English.

1 dīcit agricolās in agrīs labōrāre.

2 audiunt fēminam in viā ambulāre.

3 dīcit mīlitēs urbem novam oppugnāre.

4 audīt poētam librum tuum amāre.

5 dīcō bellum longum esse malum.

6 dīcunt nautās vīnum amāre.

7 mīles nūntiat prīncipem trāns montēs vēnisse.

8 dīcit Rōmānōs arma prope flūmen posuisse.

9 crēdimus hostēs oppidum oppugnāvisse.

10 audīmus ducem auxilium cōpiīs ferre.

Exercise 9.10

Translate into Latin:

1 He says that the farmer is working.

2 He says that the soldiers are fighting.

3 He hears that the enemy are attacking the town.

4 He hears that the enemy have attacked the town.

5 We believe* that the soldier killed the leader.

6 He says that the girl is singing.

7 They say that the woman is sleeping.

8 We believe that the master is reading a book.

9 He hears that his wife is coming.

10 We hear that the sailor is tired.

*Verbs such as crēdō, which govern an indirect object in the dative case, may be used to introduce an indirect statement just like any other verb, with the normal accusative and infinitive construction. Do not try to put 'the soldier' in the dative!

Passive tenses of the infinitive

Just as Latin has active infinitives in a number of tenses, so it has *passive* ones in a number of tenses. You already know the present infinitive passive, and the perfect passive is very easy. The future infinitive passive doesn't really exist, and we will ignore it here.

1 Present

You already know these:

amārī, monērī, regī, audīrī, capī (to be loved, to be warned, etc.)

2 Perfect

These are easily formed from the PPP, by adding esse.

E.g. amātus esse, monitus esse, rēctus esse, audītus esse, etc. (to have been loved, to have been warned, etc.)

Literally, these mean 'to be (esse) having been loved (amātus)', etc.

As you would expect, the perfect infinitive of deponent verbs is passive in form, active in meaning.

E.g. locūtus esse = to have spoken

Passive indirect statements

Using the above, we can now complete our list of indirect statements, adding the passive ones as follows:

Present: He says that the enemy **are being defeated** = dīcit hostēs **superārī**.

Perfect: He says that the enemy **have been defeated** = dīcit hostēs **superātōs esse**.

Note in this last example how the participle superātōs is agreeing with the accusative masculine plural, hostēs.

Exercise 9.11

Study the information above about passive infinitives. Then translate into English:

1 vulnerārī

2 dēfendī

3 iactus esse

4 ductus esse

5 missus esse

6 interficī

7 superātus esse

8 hortātus esse

9 datus esse

10 occīsus esse

Exercise 9.12

Translate into Latin. Don't assume that these are all passive, because they're not!

1 To be called

2 To be advised

3 To be carried

4 To have said

5 To overcome

6 To have been conquered

7 To have feared

8 To have been announced

9 To set out

10 To have set out

Exercise 9.13

Study the information above about passive indirect statements. Then translate into English:

1 dīcit urbem oppugnātam esse.

2 nūntiat mīlitēs ab hostibus interfectōs esse.

3 audiunt servum ā dominō monitum esse.

4 dīcunt nāvem tempestāte dēlētam esse.

5 audīmus multās gentēs ā Rōmānīs superātās esse.

Exercise 9.14

Translate into Latin:

1 He says that the town is being built.

2 They say that the mountains have been seen.

3 We hear that the ships were built on account of the war.

4 They announce that many gifts have been given to the citizens.

5 They say that the parents have been punished by their children.

⬤ Primary and historic tenses

Now is a good time to look again at the difference between primary and historic tenses. **Primary** tenses are: present, future, perfect, future perfect. **Historic** tenses are: imperfect, simple past and pluperfect. The imperative counts as a primary tense.

In all the examples of indirect statements that you have met so far, the verb introducing the indirect statement has been in a primary tense. But if the verb introducing the indirect statement is in a *historic* tense (e.g. 'he said' or 'we had known'), the English will adapt as follows:

Primary	Historic
He *says* that the enemy *are fighting*.	He *said* that the enemy *were fighting*.
He *says* that the enemy *will fight*.	He *said* that the enemy *would fight*.
He *says* that the enemy *have fought*.	He *said* that the enemy *had fought*.

When translating such a sentence into Latin, it may not appear obvious at first which infinitive to use. After all, there is no such thing as an imperfect infinitive, so how do we do 'were attacking' as an infinitive? Luckily there is a simple rule to follow: go back to what the words of the original direct statement would have been (e.g. 'the enemy are attacking') and use the tense of the verb there.

E.g. He *said* that the enemy *were coming* (original words: 'The enemy *are coming*') = dīxit hostēs venīre.

E.g. He *said* that the enemy *would come* (original words: 'The enemy *will come*') = dīxit hostēs ventūrōs esse.

E.g. He *said* that the enemy *had come* (original words: 'The enemy *have come*') = dīxit hostēs vēnisse.

Exercise 9.15

Study the information above about primary and historic tenses. Translate the following into English, assuming that the initial verb in each case is in a historic tense.

1 dīxit agricolās in agrīs labōrāre.

2 dīxērunt nautās ancillās amāre.

3 mīles nūntiābat Hannibalem trāns montēs vēnisse.

4 dīxit turbam prope flūmen collēctam esse.

5 crēdēbāmus hostēs oppidum mox oppugnātūrōs esse.

Exercise 9.16

Translate into Latin. Remember to go back to the original words of the direct statement to get the correct tense of the infinitive.

1 He said that the slaves were leading the horses into the field (original words: 'The slaves are leading ...').

2 They announced that the enemy had been defeated (original words: 'The enemy have been defeated').

3 She was saying that her brother had been killed in the war.

4 We heard that the rest had fled.

5 I believed that the inhabitants were fortunate.

6 He says that the girls are living at home with their mother.

7 You haven't heard that the slaves have departed, have you?

8 We heard that the poet was writing in the book.

9 He said that the slave-girl was following the master.

10 He said that the master had followed the slave.

◯ Reflexive pronouns and indirect statements

Where the subject of an indirect statement is the same as the subject of the main verb, a reflexive pronoun must be used. The 'participle bit' of the infinitive, if there is one, must agree with this pronoun, which will of course be in the accusative.

E.g. I said that **I** would come = dīxī **mē** ventūrum esse.

E.g. The Romans said that **they** (i.e. not someone else) had come = Rōmānī dīxērunt **sē** vēnisse.

If, however, the Romans said that **they** (i.e. some other people) had come, a demonstrative pronoun is used:
Rōmānī dīxērunt **eōs** vēnisse.

Reflexive pronouns can be emphasised, if required, using ipse.

E.g. He said that **he himself** had been seen = dīxit **sē ipsum** vīsum esse.

Go further

Negative indirect statements

Where an indirect statement is negative, negō, -āre = 'I deny' should be used for 'say that ... not'. Thus, instead of 'he said that he would not come', we write 'he denied that he would come'.

E.g. He said that the enemy were *not* fighting = negāvit hostēs pugnāre.

E.g. They said that they would *not* fight = negāvērunt sē pugnātūrōs esse.

Do *not* be lured into the dreadful trap of writing dīxit ... nōn!

Exercise 9.17

Study the information above about reflexive pronouns and indirect statements. Then translate into English:

1 rēx dīcēbat sē hostēs superātūrum esse.

2 agricola clāmābat sē aurum in agrō invēnisse.

3 Rōmānī nūntiāvērunt Hannibalem montēs trānsīsse.

4 puella dīcēbat sē in Ītaliam ductam esse.

5 quārtō diē dux audīvit multōs mīlitēs profectōs esse.

6 puer negāvit* sē mulierem vulnerāvisse.

7 nōnne, ō Rōmānī, vōs ipsōs semper custōdiētis?

8 dīcit cīvēs gladiīs hastīsque sē dēfendere.

9 audīvistīne rēgīnam gladiō sē interfēcisse?

10 dīxit eōs cum hostibus prō patriā pugnantēs vulnerātōs esse.

* See above on negative indirect statements.

A final thought: which accusative, which infinitive?

When translating an accusative and infinitive, it can sometimes be hard to tell which accusative to take as part of the accusative and infinitive.

E.g. dux dīxit servum mīlitem interfēcisse.

In this example, did the leader say that the slave had killed the soldier, or that the soldier had killed the slave? The normal policy is to take the first accusative first, although you will obviously have to be guided by the context.

Similarly, it can sometimes be hard to tell which infinitive to take as part of the accusative and infinitive.

E.g. mulier nūntiāvit cīvēs dōnum accipere velle.

Having established that cīvēs must be the subject of the indirect statement, do we then go to accipere or velle? Again, you need to rely on the context. However, if you remember that verbs such as volō, nōlō, possum, etc. generally govern an infinitive, this should help to explain why a sentence like this one has two infinitives.

Translate the following passage into English.

Jason undertakes a deadly task to win the golden fleece

Iasōn ad rēgem Aeētem ut vellus aureum postulāret statim contendit. hic autem, verbīs Iasōnis audītīs, vellus trādere nōlēbat. sed auxiliō deōrum sententia rēgis mūtāta est. 'vellus tibi trādam,' inquit Aeētēs, 'sed prīmō necesse est tibi duo opera difficillima suscipere.' inde Iasōnī imperāvit ut duōs taurōs, speciē horribilī,
5 quī flammās ex ōre efflābant, iungeret, et deinde, taurīs iūnctīs, agrum quendam arātum dentibus dracōnis sereret.

fīlia rēgis, nōmine Mēdēa, Iasōnem forte cōnspectum magnopere amāvit nec iuvenem illum fortissimum morī cupiēbat. itaque herbīs in montibus collēctīs Mēdēa unguentum parāvit quod Iasōnī dedit. 'hōc unguentō corpus obline,'
10 inquit, 'et tūtus eris.' hōc factō Iasōn taurōs saevōs magnā cum difficultāte cēpit et iīs iugum imposuit. tum taurōs in agrum ēgit et terram arāre coepit. ubi ager parātus est, dentēs dracōnis, quōs Aeētēs dedit, Iasōn in terrā sēvit. et ex terrā, ubi dentēs satī sunt, virī ingentēs gladiīs galeīsque armātī ortī sunt quōs ut interficeret Aeētēs Iasōnī imperāvit.

15 quamquam opus perīculōsum erat, propter auxilium Mēdēae Iason nōn timēbat. saxum enim ingēns in mediōs virōs armātōs iēcit. 'quis saxum iēcit?' inquiunt virī, inter sē clāmantēs. 'cūr nōs aggrediminī?'

aliī in aliōs ruentēs, virī armātī statim pugnāre coepērunt. mox ferōciter pugnātum est et multī sociōs aggressī interfectī sunt. quō vīsō, Iasōn cēterōs
20 facile occīdit et opus cōnfectum est.

Aeētēs, -ae, m. = Aeetes	dracō, -ōnis, m. = dragon
vellus, -eris, n. = fleece	serō, -ere, sēvī, satum = I sow
aureus, -a, -um = golden	forte = by chance
postulō, -āre = I ask for, demand	herba, -ae, f. = herb
sententia, -ae, f. = opinion	unguentum, -ī, n. = ointment
mūtō, -āre = I change	oblinō, -ere = I smear
prīmō = at first	difficultās, -ātis, f. = difficulty
necesse = necessary	iugum, -ī, n. = yoke
suscipiō, -ere = I undertake	impōnō, -ere = I place upon
taurus, -ī, m. = bull	coepī = I begin
speciēs, -ēī, f. = appearance	galea, -ae, f. = helmet
horribilis, -e = horrible	orior, orīrī, ortus sum = I arise
flamma, -ae, f. = flame	perīculōsus, -a, -um = dangerous
ōs, ōris, n. = mouth	saxum, -ī, n. = rock
efflō, -āre = I breathe out	aggredior, aggredī, aggressus sum = I attack
iungō, -ere = I join, yoke together	ferōciter = fiercely
quīdam = a certain	facile = easily
arō, -āre = I plough	cōnficiō, -ere, cōnfēcī, cōnfectum = I
dēns, dentis, m. = tooth	complete

10 Pluperfect subjunctive; cum + subjunctive; adverbs

Pluperfect subjunctive

The pluperfect subjunctive active is formed from the perfect infinitive (e.g. amāvisse) by adding -m, etc. or, if you prefer, by adding -issem, etc. to the perfect stem. The passive is the same as the indicative except that, in place of the imperfect *indicative* of sum, it uses the imperfect *subjunctive*.

Active				
amāv-issem	monu-issem	rēx-issem	audīv-issem	cēp-issem
amāv-issēs	monu-issēs	rēx-issēs	audīv-issēs	cēp-issēs
amāv-isset	monu-isset	rēx-isset	audīv-isset	cēp-isset
amāv-issēmus	monu-issēmus	rēx-issēmus	audīv-issēmus	cēp-issēmus
amāv-issētis	monu-issētis	rēx-issētis	audīv-issētis	cēp-issētis
amāv-issent	monu-issent	rēx-issent	audīv-issent	cēp-issent
Passive				
amātus essem	monitus essem	rēctus essem	audītus essem	captus essem
amātus essēs	monitus essēs	rēctus essēs	audītus essēs	captus essēs
amātus esset	monitus esset	rēctus esset	audītus esset	captus esset
amātī essēmus	monitī essēmus	rēctī essēmus	audītī essēmus	captī essēmus
amātī essētis	monitī essētis	rēctī essētis	audītī essētis	captī essētis
amātī essent	monitī essent	rēctī essent	audītī essent	captī essent

Exercise 10.1

Study the information above about the pluperfect subjunctive. Write out the pluperfect subjunctive active and passive of the following verbs:

1 trahō   2 ferō   3 portō   4 vincō

Temporal clauses

Temporal clauses refer to time. They generally have their verb in the indicative, and are introduced by the conjunctions ubi = 'when', postquam = 'after', antequam or priusquam = 'before', simul atque (or simul ac) = 'as soon as', etc.

But, after cum = 'when', the **pluperfect subjunctive** is used.

E.g. cum hoc fēcisset = When he had done this.

Go further

More on temporal clauses

1 Where a temporal clause refers to the future, in Latin a **future perfect** tense is generally used where in English we use what appears to be a present tense.

   E.g. **When you come** to Rome I will lead you into the forum (i.e. When you *will have* come to Rome, etc.) = **ubi** Rōmam **vēneris**, tē in forum dūcam.

2 After the conjunctions ubi, postquam, etc., Latin uses a **perfect** tense where in English we use a pluperfect.

   E.g. ubi hoc fēcit = When he *had* done this (or 'When he did this').

   E.g. postquam hoc audīvit = After he *had* heard this (or 'after he heard this').

3 Where some idea other than that of time is introduced (this will normally be *purpose*), the **subjunctive** is used.

   E.g. priusquam hostēs castra pōnerent, dux impetum in eōs fēcit = Before the enemy could pitch camp, the general made an attack on them.

   The idea here is that the leader attacked the enemy *with the purpose of preventing them* from pitching camp. There is thus an idea of purpose as well as of time.

Exercise 10.2

Study the information above about temporal clauses. Then translate into English. Where the Latin perfect tense is used, translate this with an English pluperfect where this sounds more natural.

1 cum Rōmānī cum Hannibale pugnāvissent, eum superāvērunt.

2 postquam Hannibal Rōmānōs vīdit, exercitum parāvit.

3 antequam cīvēs mūrum aedificārent, dux exercitum in eōs dūxit.

4 ubi domum vēnistī, templa tibi ostendī.

5 antequam domum redīstī, multās gentēs vīdistī.

6 cum templa vīdissēs, domum celeriter redīstī.

7 postquam omnia templa vīdistī, tē domum dūxī.

8 postquam domum redīstī, multa dōna mātrī patrīque dedistī.

9 ubi rēx sīc locūtus est, nōs fugere cōnstituimus.

10 cum nūntium audīvissēmus, in domum festīnāvimus.

Exercise 10.3

Translate into Latin, using temporal clauses:

1 When we saw the angry man, we immediately fled towards the fields.

2 After you had prepared the food and wine, you called us into the house.

3 When you come to our island, I will show you the temples.

4 When we found the gold, we carried it into the town.

5 Before he was able to fight, the soldier prepared his weapons.

Exercise 10.4

An ablative absolute construction is often used in place of a temporal clause. Translate the following, beginning each one with the word 'when':

1 virō vīsō, in montēs fūgimus.

2 cibō parātō, in domum nōs vocāvit.

3 hostibus superātīs, dux domum rediit.

4 mīlite interfectō, omnēs sociī fūgērunt.

5 mulieribus līberātīs, custōs sē occīdit.

Causal clauses

A causal clause gives the *cause* of the action of the main verb and is introduced in English by a word such as 'because' or 'since'.

E.g. He went to Rome *because/since* his mother lived there.

In Latin they are introduced by the conjunctions quod or quia (+ indicative) = 'because', quoniam (+ indicative) = 'since' or cum (+ subjunctive) = 'since'. If, however, only an 'alleged reason' is given, the verb *always* goes in the subjunctive.

E.g. servum interfēcit quod eum timēbat = He killed the slave because he feared him.

E.g. servum interfēcit cum eum timēret = He killed the slave since he feared him.

E.g. servum interfēcit quia eum timēret = He killed the slave, *allegedly* because he feared him.

◯ More about cum

The Latin word cum can cause all sorts of trouble if you are not careful. As you know, it can be a preposition followed by the ablative, meaning 'with' or 'together with'. But it can also be a conjunction, having a variety of meanings. So, here is a user's guide to cum:

1 cum (+ ablative) = 'with', 'together with'.
   E.g. cum amīcō ambulābam = I was walking with my friend.
2 cum (+ indicative) = 'when', referring to the present or future.
   E.g. cum hūc veniēs ... = When you come here ...
3 cum (+ imperfect subjunctive) = 'while', 'since', 'when' or 'although'.
   E.g. cum bellum in Ītaliā gereret ... = While he was waging war in Italy ...
   E.g. cum esset audāx, in proelium ruit = Since he was bold, he rushed into battle.
   E.g. patrem meum, cum mīles nōn esset, laudāvistī = You praised my father, although he was not a soldier.
4 cum (+ pluperfect subjunctive) = 'when' or 'after', referring to the past.
   E.g. cum domum revēnisset ... = When he had come back home ...'

There are other ways in which cum may be used but the ones above are by far the most common. If you master these, you should never find yourself stuck.

Exercise 10.5

Translate into English:

1 trīstis sum quod discessistī.

2 trīstis eram cum discēderēs.

3 Rōmam festīnāvit quod mātrem patremque vidēre cupīvit.

4 in domum iniit quod omnēs librōs legere volēbat.

5 in montēs iter fēcit cum Ītaliam vincere vellet.

6 incolae, cum mīlitēs appropinquārent, sē dēfendere parābant.

7 cīvēs, cum domūs tempestāte dēlētae essent, in montēs fūgērunt.

8 agricolae, cum vīnum biberent, laetī erant.

9 cum ventī saevī essent, nautae in portū semper manēbant.

10 puellam parvam, cum in templō cantāret, omnēs laudābant.

Exercise 10.6

Translate into English:

1 Poenī Hannibalem in aliam terram mīsērunt cum hostēs superāre nōn posset.

2 hic, nē ā Poenīs caperētur, ad rēgem illius terrae ībat.

3 multīs bellīs prō patriā gestīs, dux audāx ab amīcīs relictus est.

4 in oppidō rēgis superbī diū habitābat nē ā sociīs interficerētur.

5 tandem, cum mortem cuperet, dux ille fortissimus sē interfēcit.

Go further

Formation of adverbs

You have met many adverbs in this course, such as iam, mox, nunc, etc. But just as in English we can form an adverb from an adjective, often simply by adding -ly, so it is in Latin that an adverb can be formed from the adjective.

Adverbs are used to describe verbs (e.g. 'she sang beautifully'), adjectives (e.g. 'amazingly clever') and even other adverbs (e.g. 'amazingly well'). In Latin, they may be formed from adjectives as follows:

1st/2nd declension adjectives: add -ē (or occasionally -ō) to the stem:

dignus = worthy   dignē = worthily

pulcher = beautiful   pulchrē = beautifully

tūtus = safe   tūtō = safely

3rd declension adjectives: add -iter, -ter or -er to the stem:

fortis = brave   fortiter = bravely

audāx = bold   audācter = boldly

cōnstāns = steady   cōnstanter = steadily

Some adjectives simply use their neuter singular:

multus = much   multum = much, a lot

facilis = easy   facile = easily

Notes

1 The regular formation of adverbs from 1st/2nd declension adjectives is to add -ē to the stem. Those that add -ō are irregular and are not wildly common.

2 3rd declension adjectives regularly add -iter to the stem, unless the stem ends in -nt, in which case they add -er. It is pure laziness on the part of audax to go audacter, and indeed the Romans themselves didn't seem too sure whether they should be saying audacter, as audaciter is also occasionally found (although it is rare).

3 The fact that some adjectives use their neuter singular is, indeed, a blow to morale. There's nothing you can do about this one, apart from learn those adjectives that do it.

Comparison of adverbs

1 The comparative of an adverb (e.g. 'more bravely') is the same as the neuter singular of the comparative adjective.

2 The superlative of an adverb (e.g. 'very bravely' or 'most bravely') is the same as the superlative adjective but changing -us to -ē.

Thus, using the adjective laetus = 'happy' and fortis = 'brave', we can show the relationship between the adjective and the adverb as follows:

	Positive	Comparative	Superlative
Adjective:	laetus, -a, um	laetior, laetius	laetissimus, -a, –um
Adverb:	laetē	laetius	laetissimē
Adjective:	fortis, forte	fortior, fortius	fortissimus, -a, –um
Adverb:	fortiter	fortius	fortissimē

As we have seen, a very common use of the superlative adverb is in phrases after quam such as quam celerrime = as quickly as possible.

Exercise 10.7

Study the information above about the formation and comparison of adverbs. Then translate into Latin:

1 Easy, more easy, most easy

2 Easily, more easily, most easily

3 Fortunate, more fortunate, very fortunate

4 Fortunately, more fortunately, very fortunately

5 Beautiful, more beautiful, very beautiful

6 Beautifully, more beautifully, most beautifully

Exercise 10.8

Translate into Latin:

1 The young man was fighting boldly in the battle.

2 The kings ruled wisely in the city.

3 We were running more quickly than you.

4 The Romans fought more bravely than the Greeks.

5 The citizens gave the gold to the enemy as quickly as possible.

Exercise 10.9

Read the following passage and answer the questions below.

Jason and Medea join forces

postquam hunc labōrem cōnfēcit, Iāsōn ad nāvem suam contendit ut domum
redīret; nec tamen sine vellere aureō. Aeētēs autem, quī crēdēbat sē dolō
dēceptum esse, vellus eī trādere nōlēbat. Mēdēa, cum patrem magnopere
timēret, ad nāvem cum frātre parvō nōmine Absyrtō mediā nocte sē contulit
5 et Iāsōnem ōrāvit ut cum eō in Thessaliam iter facerent. ille, quod Mēdēa ūtilissima
fuerat, libenter puellam frātremque excēpit.

> cōnficiō, -ere = I complete
> vellus, velleris, n. = fleece
> aureus, -a, -um = golden
> dolus, -ī, m. = trick
> dēcipiō, -ere = I deceive
> sē cōnferre = to take oneself
> ōrō, -āre = I beg
> ūtilis, -e = useful
> libenter = gladly
> excipiō, -ere = I receive

1 postquam ... redīret (lines 1–2). What did Jason do after completing his task and why?

2 nec tamen sine vellere aureō (line 2). What did he wish to happen before he went?

3 Aeētēs ... nōlēbat (lines 2–3). Why was Aeetes unwilling to hand over the fleece?

4 Mēdēa ... sē contulit (lines 3–4). What did Medea do and what was her reason for doing this?

5 Iāsōnem ... facerent (line 5). What did Medea ask of Jason?

6 ille ... excēpit (lines 5–6). How did Jason react and what was his reason for this?

Translate into English (words glossed above are not listed again here):

Jason seizes the golden fleece

postrīdiē Iāsōn cum sociīs suīs prīmā lūce nāvem dēdūxit et ad locum ubi Mēdēa
vellus abditum esse dīxerat nāvigāvit. eō cum vēnissent Iāsōn Mēdēaque, sociīs
ad mare relictīs, in silvās prōgressī sunt. postquam pauca mīlia passuum per
silvās contendērunt, vellus ex arbore suspēnsum cōnspexērunt. hoc ā dracōne
5 custōdiēbātur nec Iāsōn id capere poterat. Mēdēa tamen, quae summam artis
magicae scientiam habēbat, rāmum venēnō īnfectum rapuit et ad dracōnem
progressa eum rāmō tetigit. quō factō dracō somnō oppressus est et Iāsōn vellus
aureum ex arbore āvellere poterat.

postrīdiē = on the next day	ars, artis, f. = art, skill
nāvem dēdūcō, -ere = I launch a ship	magicus, -a, -um = magic
abdō, -ere, abdidī, abditum = I hide	scientia, -ae, f. = knowledge
eō = (to) there	rāmus, -ī, m. = branch
silva, -ae, f. = wood	venēnum, -ī, n. = poison
mīlle passūs = a mile	īnficiō, -ere = I stain
arbor, -oris, f. = tree	rapiō, -ere, rapuī, raptum = I seize
suspendō, -ere, -pendī, -pēnsum = I hang up	tangō, -ere, tetigī, tāctum = I touch
dracō, -ōnis, m. = dragon	opprimō, -ere, oppressī, oppressum = I overpower
summus, -a, -um = topmost, utmost	āvellō, -ere = I tear down

Read the following passage and answer the questions below.

Medea shows a cruel streak

Argonautae, quī ad mare relictī erant, Iāsōnis reditum animō anxiō exspectābant.
ille enim tōtum diem āfuerat et comitēs perterritī erant. 'nōnne mortuus est?'
inquiunt. sed tandem per tenebrās veniēns lūmen cōnspexērunt et ducem suum
vellus aureum ferentem vīdērunt. magnō cum gaudiō Iāsōnem Mēdēamque in
5 nāvem accēpērunt et sine mōrā, ancorīs sublātīs, prīmā vigiliā* profectī sunt.
Aeētēs tamen, cum fīliam fīliumque abesse cognōvisset, nāvem longam dēdūcī
iussit et Argonautās fugientēs secūtus est.

Mēdēa autem, cum crēderet patrem fīlium amāre, puerum <u>crūdēliter</u> occīdit et <u>membra</u> eius in mare <u>coniēcit</u>. Aeētēs, cum <u>cōnspectum</u> <u>horribilem</u> vīdisset,
10 nautīs ut <u>cōnsisterent</u> imperāvit. <u>membra</u> enim fīliī colligere cupiēbat pater miserrimus. <u>Argonautae</u> autem, <u>vellus</u> <u>aureum</u> ferentēs, trāns mare ad Thessaliam quam celerrimē <u>regressī</u> sunt.

*The Romans divided the night up into four 'watches' of equal length, spread across the hours of darkness.

Argonautae, -ārum, m. pl. = the Argonauts	cognōscō, -ere, cognōvī, cognitum = I learn, find out
reditus, -ūs, m. = return	dedūcō = I launch (a ship)
animus, -ī, m. = mind	crūdēliter = cruelly
anxius, -a, -um = anxious	membrum, -i, n. = limb
tenebrae, -ārum, f. pl. = darkness	coniciō, -ere, coniēcī, coniectum = I throw
lūmen, -inis, n. = light	
gaudium, -ī, n. = joy	cōnspectus, -ūs, m. = sight
mōra, -ae, f. = delay	horribilis, -e, = horrible
ancorās tollō, tollere, sustulī, sublātum = I weigh anchor	cōnsistō, -ere = I halt
	regredior, -ī, regressus sum = I return, go back
vigilia, -ae, f. = watch (of the night)	

1 From the passage, give one example of each of the following:

(a) a present participle

(b) a verb in the imperfect subjunctive

(c) a verb in the pluperfect subjunctive

(d) an ablative absolute construction

(e) a deponent verb.

2 tōtum diem (line 2). Why are these words in this case?

3 veniēns (line 3). In which case is this word?

4 cognōvisset (line 6). Give the **tense** and **mood** of this verb, and explain why these are used here.

5 deducī (line 6). What part of the verb is this?

6 crēderet (line 8). Explain the **tense** and **mood** of this verb.

7 crūdēliter (line 8). What part of speech is this? How would you say in Latin 'more cruelly'?

8 quam celerrimē (line 12). Translate this phrase.

Guide to pronunciation

◯ Vowels

The main problem with learning to pronounce Latin correctly is the vowels. The Romans pronounced their vowels as follows:

ă (short)	as in cup	ā (long)	as in calf
ě (short)	as in set	ē (long)	as in stair
ĭ (short)	as in bit	ī (long)	as in bee
ŏ (short)	as in lot	ō (long)	as in the French *beau*
ŭ (short)	as in put	ū (long)	as in route

The one that looks most odd here is the short ă. It really was pronounced like the u in cup, not the a in hat.

In this book, *long* vowels are marked with a macron (ā, ē, ī, ō, ū). If they are *not* marked, they are short. Occasionally a short vowel is *marked* as short (ă, ě, ĭ, ŏ, ŭ) if there is an incorrect tendency to pronounce the vowel long. For example, the o in the Latin words egŏ and duŏ are marked as short because so many people pronounce the words as if they were long.

A vowel is regularly pronounced long when followed by ns or nf. This rule even applies across a word junction, so for example to the word in when this is followed by a word starting with s or f.

E.g. **in** agrō but **īn** suō agrō.

A few words, such as ibi, ubi and octo, end in vowels which can be pronounced long or short. In these cases, we have not marked the vowel, but in practice you will probably find it easier to pronounce the vowel as long.

◯ Diphthongs

Where two vowels are pronounced as *one* sound (as in the English *boil*, or *wait*), this is called a **diphthong** and the resulting syllable will always be long. For example the -ae at the end of the word puell**ae** is a diphthong. Diphthongs, because they are always long, are not marked with a macron.

The most common diphthongs are:
   ae   as in eye
   au   as in now

Both of these diphthongs are found in the Latin word nautae = sailors.

Where two vowels come together but are NOT a diphthong, the first vowel will always be pronounced short. Thus, the **ue** in the word p**ue**llae is not a diphthong (the word has three syllables), and the **u** is thus pronounced short: **pŭ-ell**-ae.

Consonants

- C is always 'hard' as in cot, never 'soft' as in century.
- R is always rolled.
- S is always 's' as in bus, never 'z' as in busy.
- V is pronounced as a W.
- GN is pronounced NGN, as in hangnail.
- Latin has no letter J. The Romans used i as a consonant instead (thus Iūlius Caesar, pronounced Yulius).
- M, at the end of a word, was nasalised and reduced (i.e. only partially pronounced).

Stress

Just as in English we have a particular way of stressing words, so they did in Latin. We, for example, say potáto (with the stress on the a). When we learn English words, we automatically learn how to stress them. This would have been the same for the Romans, learning Latin words.

The Romans worked out how to stress a word by looking at its penultimate syllable. Syllables are either long or short. They are long if they contain a long vowel, or if they contain a short vowel followed by two consonants. They are short if they contain a short vowel which is *not* followed by two consonants. Using this information, a Latin word should be stressed as follows:

- The final syllable of a word should never be stressed (e.g. ámō, ámās, ámat, etc.)
- In a word of more than two syllables, if the penultimate syllable is long, stress it (e.g. amātis is stressed amátis; amāvistis is stressed amāvístis).
- If the penultimate syllable is short, stress the one before it (e.g. regĭtis is stressed régitis).

Summary of grammar

Items marked with an asterisk* are only required for scholarship
(CASE) exams.

◯ Regular verbs: active voice

Present indicative: *I love, I am loving, I do love*

amō	moneō	regō	audiō	capiō
amās	monēs	regis	audīs	capis
amat	monet	regit	audit	capit
amāmus	monēmus	regimus	audīmus	capimus
amātis	monētis	regitis	audītis	capitis
amant	monent	regunt	audiunt	capiunt

Future indicative: *I shall love*

amābō	monēbō	regam	audiam	capiam
amābis	monēbis	regēs	audiēs	capiēs
amābit	monēbit	reget	audiet	capiet
amābimus	monēbimus	regēmus	audiēmus	capiēmus
amābitis	monēbitis	regētis	audiētis	capiētis
amābunt	monēbunt	regent	audient	capient

Imperfect indicative: *I was loving, I loved, I used to love*

amābam	monēbam	regēbam	audiēbam	capiēbam
amābās	monēbās	regēbās	audiēbās	capiēbās
amābat	monēbat	regēbat	audiēbat	capiēbat
amābāmus	monēbāmus	regēbāmus	audiēbāmus	capiēbāmus
amābātis	monēbātis	regēbātis	audiēbātis	capiēbātis
amābant	monēbant	regēbant	audiēbant	capiēbant

Perfect indicative: *I have loved, I loved*

amāvī	monuī	rēxī	audīvī	cēpī
amāvistī	monuistī	rēxistī	audīvistī	cēpistī
amāvit	monuit	rēxit	audīvit	cēpit
amāvimus	monuimus	rēximus	audīvimus	cēpimus
amāvistis	monuistis	rēxistis	audīvistis	cēpistis
amāvērunt	monuērunt	rēxērunt	audīvērunt	cēpērunt

Pluperfect indicative: *I had loved*

amāveram	monueram	rēxeram	audīveram	cēperam
amāverās	monuerās	rēxerās	audīverās	cēperās
amāverat	monuerat	rēxerat	audīverat	cēperat
amāverāmus	monuerāmus	rēxerāmus	audīverāmus	cēperāmus
amāverātis	monuerātis	rēxerātis	audīverātis	cēperātis
amāverant	monuerant	rēxerant	audīverant	cēperant

Imperfect subjunctive

amārem	monērem	regerem	audīrem	caperem
amārēs	monērēs	regerēs	audīrēs	caperēs
amāret	monēret	regeret	audīret	caperet
amārēmus	monērēmus	regerēmus	audīrēmus	caperēmus
amārētis	monērētis	regerētis	audīrētis	caperētis
amārent	monērent	regerent	audīrent	caperent

*Pluperfect subjunctive

amāvissem	monuissem	rēxissem	audīvissem	cēpissem
amāvissēs	monuissēs	rēxissēs	audīvissēs	cēpissēs
amāvisset	monuisset	rēxisset	audīvisset	cēpisset
amāvissēmus	monuissēmus	rēxissēmus	audīvissēmus	cēpissēmus
amāvissētis	monuissētis	rēxissētis	audīvissētis	cēpissētis
amāvissent	monuissent	rēxissent	audīvissent	cēpissent

Future perfect: *I will have loved*

amāverō	monuerō	rēxerō	audīverō	cēperō
amāveris	monueris	rēxeris	audīveris	cēperis
amāverit	monuerit	rēxerit	audīverit	cēperit
amāverimus	monuerimus	rēxerimus	audīverimus	cēperimus
amāveritis	monueritis	rēxeritis	audīveritis	cēperitis
amāverint	monuerint	rēxerint	audīverint	cēperint

◯ Regular verbs: passive voice

Present: *I am loved*

amor	moneor	regor	audior	capior
amāris	monēris	regeris	audīris	caperis
amātur	monētur	regitur	auditur	capitur
amāmur	monēmur	regimur	audīmur	capimur
amāminī	monēminī	regiminī	audīminī	capiminī
amantur	monentur	reguntur	audiuntur	capiuntur

Future: *I shall be loved*

amābor	monēbor	regar	audiar	capiar
amāberis	monēberis	regēris	audiēris	capiēris
amābitur	monēbitur	regētur	audiētur	capiētur
amābimur	monēbimur	regēmur	audiēmur	capiēmur
amābiminī	monēbiminī	regēminī	audiēminī	capiēminī
amābuntur	monēbuntur	regentur	audientur	capientur

Imperfect: *I was being loved, I was loved, I used to be loved*

amābar	monēbar	regēbar	audiēbar	capiēbar
amābāris	monēbāris	regēbāris	audiēbāris	capiēbāris
amābātur	monēbātur	regēbātur	audiēbātur	capiēbātur
amābāmur	monēbāmur	regēbāmur	audiēbāmur	capiēbāmur
amābāminī	monēbāminī	regēbāminī	audiēbāminī	capiēbāminī
amābantur	monēbantur	regēbantur	audiēbantur	capiēbantur

Perfect: *I have been loved, I was loved*

amātus sum	monitus sum	rēctus sum	audītus sum	captus sum
amātus es	monitus es	rēctus es	audītus es	captus es
amātus est	monitus est	rēctus est	audītus est	captus est
amātī sumus	monitī sumus	rēctī sumus	audītī sumus	captī sumus
amātī estis	monitī estis	rēctī estis	audītī estis	captī estis
amātī sunt	monitī sunt	rēctī sunt	audītī sunt	captī sunt

Pluperfect: *I had been loved*

amātus eram	monitus eram	rēctus eram	audītus eram	captus eram
amātus erās	monitus erās	rēctus erās	audītus erās	captus erās
amātus erat	monitus erat	rēctus erat	audītus erat	captus erat
amātī erāmus	monitī erāmus	rēctī erāmus	audītī erāmus	captī erāmus
amātī erātis	monitī erātis	rēctī erātis	audītī erātis	captī erātis
amātī erant	monitī erant	rēctī erant	audītī erant	captī erant

Imperfect subjunctive

amārer	monērer	regerer	audīrer	caperer
amārēris	monērēris	regerēris	audīrēris	caperēris
amārētur	monērētur	regerētur	audīrētur	caperētur
amārēmur	monērēmur	regerēmur	audīrēmur	caperēmur
amārēminī	monērēminī	regerēminī	audīrēminī	caperēminī
amārentur	monērentur	regerentur	audīrentur	caperentur

Go further

Future perfect: *I will have been loved*

amātus erō	monitus erō	rēctus erō	audītus erō	captus erō
amātus eris	monitus eris	rēctus eris	audītus eris	captus eris
amātus erit	monitus erit	rēctus erit	audītus erit	captus erit
amātī erimus	monitī erimus	rēctī erimus	audītī erimus	captī erimus
amātī eritis	monitī eritis	rēctī eritis	audītī eritis	captī eritis
amātī erunt	monitī erunt	rēctī erunt	audītī erunt	captī erunt

◯ Imperatives, infinitives and participles

Imperative: *Love!*

amā	monē	regĕ	audī	capĕ
amāte	monēte	regĭte	audīte	capĭte

Present infinitive active: *To love*

amāre	monēre	regere	audīre	capere

***Present infinitive passive:** *To be loved*

amārī	monērī	regī	audīrī	capī

***Perfect infinitive active:** *To have loved*

amāvisse	monuisse	rēxisse	audīvisse	cēpisse

***Perfect infinitive passive:** *To have been loved*

amātus esse	monitus esse	rēctus esse	audītus esse	captus esse

Present participle active: *Loving*

amāns	monēns	regēns	audiēns	capiēns

Perfect participle passive: *Having been loved*

amātus	monitus	rēctus	audītus	captus

◯ Irregular verbs: sum, esse, fuī = *I am*; possum, posse, potuī = *I am able*; eō, īre, iī = *I go*

Present

sum	possum	eō
es	potes	īs
est	potest	it
sumus	possumus	īmus
estis	potestis	ītis
sunt	possunt	eunt

Future

erō	poterō	ibō
eris	poteris	ibis
erit	poterit	ibit
erimus	poterimus	ibimus
eritis	poteritis	ibitis
erunt	poterunt	ibunt

Imperfect

eram	poteram	ibam
erās	poterās	ibās
erat	poterat	ibat
erāmus	poterāmus	ibāmus
erātis	poterātis	ibātis
erant	poterant	ibant

Perfect

fuī	potuī	iī/īvī
fuistī	potuistī	īstī/īvistī
fuit	potuit	iit/īvit
fuimus	potuimus	iimus/īvimus
fuistis	potuistis	īstis/īvistis
fuērunt	potuērunt	iērunt/īverunt

Imperfect subjunctive

essem	possem	īrem
essēs	possēs	īrēs
esset	posset	īret
essēmus	possēmus	īrēmus
essētis	possētis	īrētis
essent	possent	īrent

Imperatives

es	–	ī
este	–	ite

Present infinitive active

esse   posse   īre

*Perfect infinitive active

fuisse   potuisse   īsse/īvisse

Present participle

–   –   iens, euntis

◯ Irregular verbs: ferō, ferre, tulī, latum = I carry; volō, velle, voluī = I am willing; nōlō, nōlle, nōluī = I am unwilling

Present

ferō	volō	nōlō
fers	vīs	nōn vīs
fert	vult	nōn vult
ferimus	volumus	nōlumus
fertis	vultis	nōn vultis
ferunt	volunt	nōlunt

Future

feram	volam	nōlam
ferēs	volēs	nōlēs
feret	volet	nōlet
ferēmus	volēmus	nōlēmus
ferētis	volētis	nōlētis
ferent	volent	nōlent

Imperfect

ferēbam	volēbam	nōlēbam
ferēbās	volēbās	nōlēbās
ferēbat	volēbat	nōlēbat
ferēbāmus	volēbāmus	nōlēbāmus
ferēbātis	volēbātis	nōlēbātis
ferēbant	volēbant	nōlēbant

Perfect

tulī	voluī	nōluī
tulistī	voluistī	nōluistī
tulit	voluit	nōluit
tulimus	voluimus	nōluimus
tulistis	voluistis	nōluistis
tulērunt	voluērunt	nōluērunt

Imperfect subjunctive

ferrem	vellem	nōllem
ferrēs	vellēs	nōllēs
ferret	vellet	nōllet
ferrēmus	vellēmus	nōllēmus
ferrētis	vellētis	nōllētis
ferrent	vellent	nōllent

Imperatives

fer	–	nōlī
ferte	–	nōlīte

Present infinitive active

ferre	velle	nōlle

Perfect infinitive active

tulisse	voluisse	nōluisse

Present Participle

ferēns	volēns	(nolēns)

Of the irregular verbs above, only ferō is found in the passive.

ferō: passive forms

Present passive	Future passive	Imperfect
feror	ferar	ferēbar
ferris	ferēris	ferēbāris
fertur	ferētur	ferēbātur
ferimur	ferēmur	ferēbāmur
feriminī	ferēminī	ferēbāminī
feruntur	ferentur	ferēbantur

Perfect passive	Imperfect subjunctive passive
lātus sum	ferrer
lātus es	ferrēris
lātus est	ferrētur
lātī sumus	ferrēmur
lātī estis	ferrēminī
lātī sunt	ferrentur

◯ Nouns

1st declension

Nominative	puella	Girl (subject)
Vocative	puella	O girl
Accusative	puellam	Girl (object)
Genitive	puellae	Of a girl
Dative	puellae	To, for a girl
Ablative	puellā	With, by or from a girl
Nominative	puellae	Girls (subject)
Vocative	puellae	O girls
Accusative	puellās	Girls (object)
Genitive	puellārum	Of the girls
Dative	puellīs	To, for the girls
Ablative	puellīs	With, by or from the girls

2nd declension

Nominative	dominus	puer	magister	bellum
Vocative	domine	puer	magister	bellum
Accusative	dominum	puerum	magistrum	bellum
Genitive	dominī	puerī	magistrī	bellī
Dative	dominō	puerō	magistrō	bellō
Ablative	dominō	puerō	magistrō	bellō
Nominative	dominī	puerī	magistrī	bella
Vocative	dominī	puerī	magistrī	bella
Accusative	dominōs	puerōs	magistrōs	bella
Genitive	dominōrum	puerōrum	magistrōrum	bellōrum
Dative	dominīs	puerīs	magistrīs	bellīs
Ablative	dominīs	puerīs	magistrīs	bellīs

2nd declension irregular

Nominative	fīlius	deus	vir
Vocative	fīlī	deus	vir
Accusative	fīlium	deum	virum
Genitive	fīliī (fīlī)	deī	virī
Dative	fīliō	deō	virō
Ablative	fīliō	deō	virō
Nominative	fīliī	dī (deī)	virī
Vocative	fīliī	dī (deī)	virī
Accusative	fīliōs	deōs	virōs
Genitive	fīliōrum	deōrum (deum)	virōrum (virum)
Dative	fīliīs	dīs (deīs)	virīs
Ablative	fīliīs	dīs (deīs)	virīs

3rd declension: increasing

	M/F	N
Nominative	rēx	corpus
Vocative	rēx	corpus
Accusative	rēgem	corpus
Genitive	rēgis	corporis
Dative	rēgī	corporī
Ablative	rēge	corpore
Nominative	rēgēs	corpora
Vocative	rēgēs	corpora
Accusative	rēgēs	corpora
Genitive	rēgum	corporum
Dative	rēgibus	corporibus
Ablative	rēgibus	corporibus

3rd declension: non-increasing

	M/F	N
Nominative	cīvis	mare
Vocative	cīvis	mare
Accusative	cīvem	mare
Genitive	cīvis	maris
Dative	cīvī	marī
Ablative	cīve	marī
Nominative	cīvēs	maria
Vocative	cīvēs	maria
Accusative	cīvēs	maria
Genitive	cīvium	marium
Dative	cīvibus	maribus
Ablative	cīvibus	maribus

*4th declension

	M/F	N
Nominative	gradus	genū
Vocative	gradus	genū
Accusative	gradum	genū
Genitive	gradūs	genūs
Dative	graduī	genuī
Ablative	gradū	genū
Nominative	gradūs	genua
Vocative	gradūs	genua
Accusative	gradūs	genua
Genitive	graduum	genuum
Dative	gradibus	genibus
Ablative	gradibus	genibus

(A tiny number of 4th declension nouns are neuter, and decline like genū above.)

5th declension

Nominative	rēs	diēs
Vocative	rēs	diēs
Accusative	rem	diem
Genitive	reī	diēī
Dative	reī	diēī
Ablative	rē	diē
Nominative	rēs	diēs
Vocative	rēs	diēs
Accusative	rēs	diēs
Genitive	rērum	diērum
Dative	rēbus	diēbus
Ablative	rēbus	diēbus

Adjectives

1st/2nd declension in -us

	M	F	N
Nominative	bonus	bona	bonum
Vocative	bone	bona	bonum
Accusative	bonum	bonam	bonum
Genitive	bonī	bonae	bonī
Dative	bonō	bonae	bonō
Ablative	bonō	bonā	bonō
Nominative	bonī	bonae	bona
Vocative	bonī	bonae	bona
Accusative	bonōs	bonās	bona
Genitive	bonōrum	bonārum	bonōrum
Dative	bonīs	bonīs	bonīs
Ablative	bonīs	bonīs	bonīs

1st/2nd declension in -er

	M	F	N
Nominative	miser	misera	miserum
Vocative	miser	misera	miserum
Accusative	miserum	miseram	miserum
Genitive	miserī	miserae	miserī
Dative	miserō	miserae	miserō
Ablative	miserō	miserā	miserō
Nominative	miserī	miserae	misera
Vocative	miserī	miserae	misera
Accusative	miserōs	miserās	misera
Genitive	miserōrum	miserārum	miserōrum
Dative	miserīs	miserīs	miserīs
Ablative	miserīs	miserīs	miserīs

	M	F	N
Nominative	pulcher	pulchra	pulchrum
Vocative	pulcher	pulchra	pulchrum
Accusative	pulchrum	pulchram	pulchrum
Genitive	pulchrī	pulchrae	pulchrī
Dative	pulchrō	pulchrae	pulchrō
Ablative	pulchrō	pulchrā	pulchrō
Nominative	pulchrī	pulchrae	pulchra
Vocative	pulchrī	pulchrae	pulchra
Accusative	pulchrōs	pulchrās	pulchra
Genitive	pulchrōrum	pulchrārum	pulchrōrum
Dative	pulchrīs	pulchrīs	pulchrīs
Ablative	pulchrīs	pulchrīs	pulchrīs

3rd declension: one termination

	M	F	N
Nominative	ingēns	ingēns	ingēns
Vocative	ingēns	ingēns	ingēns
Accusative	ingentem	ingentem	ingēns
Genitive	ingentis	ingentis	ingentis
Dative	ingentī	ingentī	ingentī
Ablative	ingentī	ingentī	ingentī
Nominative	ingentēs	ingentēs	ingentia
Vocative	ingentēs	ingentēs	ingentia
Accusative	ingentēs	ingentēs	ingentia
Genitive	ingentium	ingentium	ingentium
Dative	ingentibus	ingentibus	ingentibus
Ablative	ingentibus	ingentibus	ingentibus

3rd declension: two termination

	M	F	N
Nominative	trīstis	trīstis	trīste
Vocative	trīstis	trīstis	trīste
Accusative	trīstem	trīstem	trīste
Genitive	trīstis	trīstis	trīstis
Dative	trīstī	trīstī	trīstī
Ablative	trīstī	trīstī	trīstī
Nominative	trīstēs	trīstēs	trīstia
Vocative	trīstēs	trīstēs	trīstia
Accusative	trīstēs	trīstēs	trīstia
Genitive	trīstium	trīstium	trīstium
Dative	trīstibus	trīstibus	trīstibus
Ablative	trīstibus	trīstibus	trīstibus

3rd declension: three termination

	M	F	N
Nominative	celer	celeris	celere
Vocative	celer	celeris	celere
Accusative	celerem	celerem	celere
Genitive	celeris	celeris	celeris
Dative	celerī	celerī	celerī
Ablative	celerī	celerī	celerī
Nominative	celerēs	celerēs	celeria
Vocative	celerēs	celerēs	celeria
Accusative	celerēs	celerēs	celeria
Genitive	celerium	celerium	celerium
Dative	celeribus	celeribus	celeribus
Ablative	celeribus	celeribus	celeribus

Comparative adjectives

	M	F	N
Nominative	melior	melior	melius
Vocative	melior	melior	melius
Accusative	meliōrem	meliōrem	melius
Genitive	meliōris	meliōris	meliōris
Dative	meliōrī	meliōrī	meliōrī
Ablative	meliōre	meliōre	meliōre
Nominative	meliōrēs	meliōrēs	meliōra
Vocative	meliōrēs	meliōrēs	meliōra
Accusative	meliōrēs	meliōrēs	meliōra
Genitive	meliōrum	meliōrum	meliōrum
Dative	meliōribus	meliōribus	meliōribus
Ablative	meliōribus	meliōribus	meliōribus

Personal and reflexive pronouns

Nominative	egŏ	tū	nōs	vōs	–
Accusative	mē	tē	nōs	vōs	sē
Genitive	mei	tui	nostrum	vestrum	suī
Dative	mihi	tibi	nōbīs	vōbīs	sibi
Ablative	mē	tē	nōbīs	vōbīs	sē

Demonstrative pronouns

is, ea, id = that (he, she, it)

	M	F	N
Nominative	is	ea	id
Accusative	eum	eam	id
Genitive	eius	eius	eius
Dative	eī	eī	eī
Ablative	eō	eā	eō

	M	F	N
Nominative	eī	eae	ea
Accusative	eōs	eās	ea
Genitive	eōrum	eārum	eōrum
Dative	eīs	eīs	eīs
Ablative	eīs	eīs	eīs

hic, haec, hoc = this (near me) [plural = these]

	M	F	N
Nominative	hic	haec	hoc
Accusative	hunc	hanc	hoc
Genitive	huius	huius	huius
Dative	huic	huic	huic
Ablative	hōc	hāc	hōc
Nominative	hī	hae	haec
Accusative	hōs	hās	haec
Genitive	hōrum	hārum	hōrum
Dative	hīs	hīs	hīs
Ablative	hīs	hīs	hīs

ille, illa, illud = that (over there) [plural = those]

	M	F	N
Nominative	ille	illa	illud
Accusative	illum	illam	illud
Genitive	illius	illius	illius
Dative	illī	illī	illī
Ablative	illō	illā	illō
Nominative	illī	illae	illa
Accusative	illōs	illās	illa
Genitive	illōrum	illārum	illōrum
Dative	illīs	illīs	illīs
Ablative	illīs	illīs	illīs

Relative pronoun

quī, quae, quod = who

	M	F	N
Nominative	quī	quae	quod
Accusative	quem	quam	quod
Genitive	cuius	cuius	cuius
Dative	cui	cui	cui
Ablative	quō	quā	quō
Nominative	quī	quae	quae
Accusative	quōs	quās	quae
Genitive	quōrum	quārum	quōrum
Dative	quibus/quīs	quibus/quīs	quibus/quīs
Ablative	quibus/quīs	quibus/quīs	quibus/quīs

Intensive pronoun

ipse = self

	M	F	N
Nominative	ipse	ipsa	ipsum
Accusative	ipsum	ipsam	ipsum
Genitive	ipsius	ipsius	ipsius
Dative	ipsī	ipsī	ipsī
Ablative	ipsō	ipsā	ipsō
Nominative	ipsī	ipsae	ipsa
Accusative	ipsōs	ipsās	ipsa
Genitive	ipsōrum	ipsārum	ipsōrum
Dative	ipsīs	ipsīs	ipsīs
Ablative	ipsīs	ipsīs	ipsīs

Definitive pronoun

īdem = same

	M	F	N
Nominative	īdem	eadem	idem
Accusative	eundem	eandem	idem
Genitive	eiusdem	eiusdem	eiusdem
Dative	eīdem	eīdem	eīdem
Ablative	eōdem	eādem	eōdem
Nominative	īdem/eīdem	eaedem	eadem
Accusative	eōsdem	eāsdem	eadem
Genitive	eōrundem	eārundem	eōrundem
Dative	īsdem/eīsdem	īsdem/eīsdem	īsdem/eīsdem
Ablative	īsdem/eīsdem	īsdem/eīsdem	īsdem/eīsdem

Cardinal numerals

1	I	ūnus
2	II	duŏ
3	III	trēs
4	IV/IIII	quattuor
5	V	quīnque
6	VI	sex
7	VII	septem
8	VIII	octo
9	IX	novem
10	X	decem
11	XI	ūndecim
12	XII	duodecim
13	XIII	tredecim
14	XIV	quattuordecim
15	XV	quīndecim
16	XVI	sēdecim
17	XVII	septendecim
18	XVIII	duodēvīgintī

19	XIX	ūndēvīgintī
20	XX	vīgintī
30	XXX	trīgintā
40	XL	quadrāgintā
50	L	quīnquāgintā
60	LX	sexāgintā
70	LXX	septuāgintā
80	LXXX	octōgintā
90	XC	nōnāgintā
100	C	centum
1000	M	mīlle

◯ Ordinals

1st	prīmus	6th	sextus
2nd	secundus	7th	septimus
3rd	tertius	8th	octāvus
4th	quārtus	9th	nōnus
5th	quīntus	10th	decimus

◯ Declining numerals

	Masc.	Fem.	Neut.
Nom.	ūnus	ūna	ūnum
Acc.	ūnum	ūnam	ūnum
Gen.	ūnius	ūnius	ūnius
Dat.	ūnī	ūnī	ūnī
Nom.	duŏ	duae	duŏ
Acc.	duōs/duŏ	duās	duŏ
Gen.	duōrum	duārum	duōrum
Dat.	duōbus	duābus	duōbus
Abl.	duōbus	duābus	duōbus
Nom.	trēs	trēs	tria
Acc.	trēs	trēs	tria
Gen.	trium	trium	trium
Dat.	tribus	tribus	tribus
Abl.	tribus	tribus	tribus

Latin – English vocabulary

ā/ab (+ abl.) = by, from
absum, abesse, āfuī = I am absent
accipiō, -ere, accēpī, acceptum = I receive
ad (+ acc.) = to, towards
adeō, adīre, adiī, aditum = I approach
adsum, adesse, adfuī = I am present
adveniō, -īre, advēnī, adventum = I arrive
aedificō, -āre, -āvī, -ātum = I build
āfuī: see absum
ager, agrī, m. = field
agricola, -ae, m. = farmer
alius, alia, aliud = other, another
alter, altera, alterum = other (of two)
altus, -a, -um = high, deep
amīcus, amīcī, m. = friend
amō, -āre, -āvī, -ātum = I love, like
ancilla, -ae, f. = slave-girl
animal, animālis, n. = animal
annus, -ī, m. = year
ante (+ acc.) = before
antequam = before
appropinquō, -āre, -āvī, -ātum = I approach
aqua, -ae, f. = water
arma, -ōrum, n. pl. = weapons, arms
audāx, audācis = bold
audiō, audīre, audīvī, audītum = I hear
aurum, -ī, n. = gold
aut = or
autem = however, moreover
auxilium, -iī, n. = help
bellum, bellī, n. = war
bene = well
bibō, bibere, bibī = I drink
bonus, -a, -um = good
caelum, -ī, n. = sky
cantō, -āre, -āvī, -ātum = I sing
capiō, -ere, cēpī, captum = I capture, take
cārus, -a, -um = dear
celer, celeris, celere = swift, quick
celeriter = quickly
centum = one hundred
cēpī: see capiō
cēterī, -ae, -a = the rest, others
cibus, cibī, m. = food
circum (+ acc.) = around
cīvis, cīvis, c. = citizen

clāmō, -āre, -āvī, -ātum = I shout
clāmor, clāmōris, m. = shout
clārus, -a, -um = famous, clear, bright
cōgō, cōgere, coēgī, coāctum = I compel, force
collēctum: see colligō
colligō, -ere, collēgī, collēctum = I collect
comes, comitis, c. = companion
coniūnx, coniugis, c. = husband, wife
conor, -ārī, conātus sum = I try
cōnspiciō, -ere, cōnspexī, cōnspectum = I catch sight of
cōnstituō, -ere, cōnstituī, cōnstitūtum = I decide
cōnsūmō, -ere, cōnsūmpsī, cōnsūmptum = I eat
contendō, contendere, contendī, contentum = I hurry, march, strive
contrā (+ acc.) = against
conveniō, -īre, convēnī, conventum = I meet, come together
cōpiae, -ārum, f. pl. = forces
corpus, corporis, n. = body
crās = tomorrow
crēdō, -ere, crēdidī, crēditum (+ dat.) = I trust, believe
crūdēlis, -e = cruel
cum (+ abl.) = with
cum (+ pluperfect subjunctive) = when, after
cum (+ imperfect subjunctive) = while, since, when, although
cupiō, -ere, cupīvī, cupītum = I want, desire
cūr? = why?
currō, currere, cucurrī, cursum = I run
custōdiō, -īre, -īvī, -ītum = I guard
custōs, custōdis, m. = guard
dare: see dō
datum: see dō
dē (+ abl.) = down from, concerning
dea, -ae, f. = goddess (dat. and abl. pl. = deābus)
dēbeō, -ēre, dēbuī, dēbitum = I owe, ought
decem = ten
decimus, -a, -um = tenth
dedī: see dō
dēfendō, -ere, dēfendī, dēfēnsum = I defend
deinde = then
dēleō, -ēre, dēlēvī, dēlētum = I destroy
deus, deī, m. = god
dīcō, dīcere, dīxī, dictum = I say

diēs, diēī, m. = day (fem. if an appointed day)
difficilis, -e = difficult
discēdō, -ere, discessī, discessum = I depart
diū = for a long time
dō, dăre, dedī, dătum = I give
dominus, dominī, m. = lord, master
domus, -ūs, f. = house
dōnum, -ī, n. = gift
dormiō, -īre, -īvī, -ītum = I sleep
dūcō, dūcere, dūxī, ductum = I lead
dum = while
duŏ = two
duodecim = twelve
duodēvīgintī = eighteen
dux, ducis, m. = leader
dūxī: see dūcō
ea: see is
eadem: see īdem
ē/ex (+ abl.) = out of
effugiō, -ere, effūgī = I escape
egŏ = I
ēgredior, ēgredī, ēgressus sum = I go out
eō, īre, iī/īvī, itum = I go
equus, equī, m. = horse
errō, -āre, -āvī, -ātum = I wander
et = and
et ... et = both ... and
etiam = also, even
exeō, exīre, exiī, exitum = I go out
exercitus, -ūs, m. = army
exspectō, -āre, -āvī, -ātum = I wait for
facilis, -e = easy
faciō, -ere, fēcī, factum = I do, make
fēlīx, fēlīcis = fortunate
fēmina, -ae, f. = woman
ferō, ferre, tulī, lātum (irreg.) = I carry, bear
fessus, -a, -um = tired
festīnō, -āre, -āvī, -ātum = I hurry
fidēs, fideī, f. = trust, faith, promise
fīlia, -ae, f. = daughter (dat. and abl. pl. = fīliābus)
fīlius, fīliī, m. = son
flūmen, flūminis, n. = river
forte = by chance
fortis, -e = brave, strong
fortiter = bravely
frāter, frātris, m. = brother
frūstrā = in vain
fugiō, -ere, fūgī, fugitum = I flee
gēns, gentis, f. = people, race, tribe

gerō, -ere, gessī, gestum = I carry on, wear
gladius, gladiī, m. = sword
Graecus, -a, -um = Greek
habeō, -ēre, habuī, habitum = I have
habitō, -āre, -āvī, -ātum = I live (in)
hasta, -ae, f. = spear
herī = yesterday
hīc = here
hic, haec, hoc = this
homō, hominis, m. = man, woman
hōra, -ae, f. = hour
hortor, -ārī, hortātus sum = I encourage, urge
hostis, hostis, c. = enemy
iaciō, -ere, iēcī, iactum = I throw
iam = now, already
ibi = there
īdem, eadem, idem = the same
iēcī: see iaciō
igitur = therefore
ille, illa, illud = that
impero, -āre, -āvī, -ātum (+ dat.) = I order
in (+ abl.) = in, on
in (+ acc.) = into, on to
incola, -ae, c. = inhabitant
ineō, inīre, iniī, initum = I go in
ingēns, ingentis = huge
ingredior, ingredī, ingressus sum = I go in, enter
inquit/inquiunt = he/she/they says
īnsula, -ae, f. = island
inter (+ acc.) = between, among
intereā = meanwhile
interficiō, -ere, interfēcī, interfectum = I kill
intrō, -āre, -āvī, -ātum = I enter
inveniō, -īre, invēnī, inventum = I find
ipse, ipsa, ipsum = self
īra, -ae, f. = anger
īrātus, -a, -um = angry
is, ea, id = that
itaque = therefore
iter, itineris, n. = journey
iterum = again
itineris: see iter
iubeō, -ēre, iussī, iussum = I order
iūtum: see iuvō
iuvenis, iuvenis, c. = young man, young person
iuvō, iuvāre, iūvī, iūtum = I help
labor, labōris, m. = work, task
labōrō, -āre, -āvī, -ātum = I work
laetus, -a, -um = happy

lātum: see ferō
laudō, -āre, -āvī, -ātum = I praise
legō, legere, lēgī, lectum = I read, choose
lentē = slowly
liber, librī, m. = book
līberī, -ōrum, m. pl. = children
līberō, -āre, -āvī, -ātum = I free
locus, -ī, m. = place
locūtus sum: see loquor
longus, -a, -um = long
loquor, loquī, locūtus sum = I speak
lūcis: see lūx
lūdō, -ere, lūsī, lūsum = I play
lūx, lūcis, f. = light
magister, magistrī, m. = master
magnopere = greatly, very much
magnus, -a, -um = big, great
malus, -a, -um = bad
maneō, -ēre, mānsī, mānsum = I remain
manus, -ūs, f. = hand
mare, maris, n. = sea
māter, mātris, f. = mother
medius, -a, -um = middle
mīles, mīlitis, m. = soldier
mīlle = one thousand
miser, misera, miserum = miserable, wretched,
    unhappy
mittō, mittere, mīsī, missum = I send
moneō, -ēre, monuī, monitum = I warn, advise
mōns, montis, m. = mountain
mōra, -ae, f. = delay
morior, morī, mortuus sum = I die
mors, mortis, f. = death
mortuus, -a, -um = dead
moveō, -ēre, mōvī, mōtum = I move
mox = soon
mulier, mulieris, f. = woman
multus, -a, -um = much, many
mūrus, mūrī, m. = wall
nam = for
nārrō, -āre, -āvī, -ātum = I tell, relate
nauta, -ae, m. = sailor
nāvigō, -āre, -āvī, -ātum = I sail
nāvis, nāvis, f. = ship
-ne...?: asks a question
ne (+ subjunctive) = lest, in order that ... not
nec = and not, nor
necō, -āre, -āvī, -ātum = I kill
nēmō, nūllius, c. = no one

neque = and not, nor
nihil = nothing
nōbilis, -e = noble
noctis: see nox
nōlī/nōlīte (+ infin.) = do not ...
nōlō, nōlle, nōluī = I am not willing, do not wish
nōmen, nōminis, n. = name
nōn = not
nōnāgintā = ninety
nōnne? – introduces a question expecting the
    answer 'yes'
nōnus, -a, -um = ninth
nōs = we
noster, nostra, nostrum = our
nōtus, -a, -um = well-known
novem = nine
novus, -a, -um = new
nox, noctis, f. = night
nullius: see nēmō
num? – introduces a question expecting the answer
    'no'
numquam = never
nunc = now
nūntiō, -āre, -āvī, -ātum = I report, announce
nūntius, nūntiī, m. = messenger
occīdō, -ere, occīdī, occīsum = I kill
occupō, -āre, -āvī, -ātum = I seize (a place)
octāvus, -a, -um = eighth
octo = eight
octōgintā = eighty
ōlim = once upon a time
omnis, -e = all, every
operis: see opus
oppidum, oppidī, n. = town
oppugnō, -āre, -āvī, -ātum = I attack
opus, operis, n. = work
ostendō, -ere, ostendī, ostentum = I show
paene = almost
parēns, parentis, c. = parent
parō, -āre, -āvī, -ātum = I prepare
pars, partis, f. = part
parvus, -a, -um = small
passus: see patior
pater, patris, m. = father
patior, patī, passus sum = I suffer, allow
patria, -ae, f. = country, fatherland
paucī, -ae, -a = few
pellō, -ere, pepulī, pulsum = I drive
per (+ acc.) = through

pereō, -īre, -iī, -itum = I die, perish

perīculum, perīculī, n. = danger

persuādeō, -ēre, persuāsī, persuāsum (+ dat.) = I persuade

perterritus, -a, -um = terrified

petō, -ere, petīvī, petītum = I seek, make for

Poenus, -a, -um = Carthaginian

poēta, -ae, m. = poet

pōnō, -ere, posuī, positum = I place

portō, -āre, -āvī, -ātum = I carry

portus, -ūs, m. = harbour

positum: see pōnō

possum, posse, potuī = I am able

post (+ acc.) = after

posteā = afterwards

postquam = after

posuī: see pōnō

potuī: see possum

praemium, -iī, n. = reward

prīmus, -a, -um = first

prīnceps, prīncipis, c. = chief, leader

prō (+ abl.) = on behalf of, in place of, in front of

proelium, -iī, n. = battle

proficīscor, proficīscī, profectus sum = I set out

prōgredior, prōgredī, prōgressus sum = I advance

prope (+ acc.) = near

propter (+ acc.) = on account of

puella, -ae, f. = girl

puer, puerī, m. = boy

pugnō, -āre, -āvī, -ātum = I fight

pulcher, pulchra, pulchrum = beautiful

pulsum: see pellō

pūniō, -īre, pūnīvī, pūnītum = I punish

quadrāgintā = forty

quam = how

quamquam = although

quārtus, -a, -um = fourth

quattuor = four

quattuordecim = fourteen

-que = and

quid? = what?

quīndecim = fifteen

quīnque = five

quīntus, -a, -um = fifth

quis? = who?

quod = because

quoque = also

rectum: see regō

redeō, -īre, -iī, -itum = I go back

redūcō, -ere, redūxī, reductum = I lead back

rēgīna, -ae, f. = queen

regō, regere, rēxī, rēctum = I rule

relinquō, -ere, relīquī, relictum = I leave

rēs, reī, f. = thing, affair

respondeō, -ēre, respondī, respōnsum = I answer

rēx, rēgis, m. = king

rēxī: see regō

rīdeō, -ēre, rīsī, rīsum = I laugh

rogō, -āre, -āvī, -ātum = I ask

Rōmānus, -a, -um = Roman

ruō, -ere, ruī, rutum = I rush

sacer, sacra, sacrum = sacred

saepe = often

saevus, -a, -um = savage

sagitta, -ae, f. = arrow

salūtō, -āre, -āvī, -ātum = I greet

sapiēns, sapientis = wise

scrībō, -ere, scrīpsī, scriptum = I write

scūtum, scūtī, n. = shield

sē (reflexive) = himself, herself, itself, themselves

secundus, -a, -um = second

secūtus sum: see sequor

sed = but

sēdecim = sixteen

semper = always

senex, senis, m. = old man

septem = seven

septendecim = seventeen

septimus, -a, -um = seventh

septuāgintā = seventy

sequor, sequī, secūtus sum = I follow

servō, -āre, -āvī, -ātum = I save

servus, servī, m. = slave

sex = six

sexāgintā = sixty

sextus, -a, -um = sixth

sīc = so, thus

sine (+ abl.) = without

socius, -iī, m. = companion, ally

sōlus, -a, -um = alone

somnus, -ī, m. = sleep

soror, sorōris, f. = sister

spectō, -āre, -āvī, -ātum = I watch

spēs, speī, f. = hope

statim = immediately

stō, -āre, stetī, stătum = I stand

sub (+ abl.) = under

subitō = suddenly

sum, esse, fuī = I am
super (+ acc.) = over
superbus, -a, -um = proud
superō, -āre, -āvī, -ātum = I overcome
suus, -a, -um = his own, her own, its own, their own
tamen = however
tandem = at last
tēlum, -ī, n. = spear, missile
tempestās, -ātis, f. = storm, weather
templum, -ī, n. = temple
teneō, -ēre, tenuī, tentum = I hold
terra, -ae, f. = land, ground
terreō, -ēre, terruī, territum = I frighten
tertius, -a, -um = third
timeō, -ēre, timuī = I fear
tōtus, -a, -um (goes like ūnus) = whole
trādō, -ere, trādidī, trāditum = I hand over
trāns (+ acc.) = across
trānseō, -īre, -iī, -itum = I go across
tredecim = thirteen
trēs = three
trīgintā = thirty
trīstis, -e = sad
Troiānus, -a, -um = Trojan
tū = you (sing.)
tulī: see ferō
tum = then
turba, -ae, f. = crowd
tūtus, -a, -um = safe
tuus, -a, -um = your (of you (sing.))
ubi = when
ubi? = where?

unda, -ae, f. = wave
ūndecim = eleven
ūndēvīgintī = nineteen
ūnus = one
urbs, urbis, f. = city
ut (+ subjunctive) = in order to
uxor, uxōris, f. = wife
validus, -a, -um = strong
velle: see volō
veniō, venīre, vēnī, ventum = I come
ventus, -ī, m. = wind
verbum, verbī, n. = word
vester, vestra, vestrum = your (of you (pl.))
via, -ae, f. = road, street, way
victum: see vincō
videō, -ēre, vīdī, vīsum = I see
vīgintī = twenty
vincō, -ere, vīcī, victum = I conquer
vīnum, -ī, n. = wine
vir, virī, m. = man
virtus, virtūtis, f. = courage
vīsum: see videō
vīvus, -a, -um = alive
vocō, -āre, -āvī, -ātum = I call
volō, velle, voluī = I am willing, wish
vōs = you (pl.)
vōx, vōcis, f. = voice
vulnerō, -āre, -āvī, -ātum = I wound
vulnus, vulneris, n. = wound

English – Latin vocabulary

Able, I am = possum, posse, potuī
About (concerning) = dē (+ abl.)
Absent, I am = absum, abesse, āfuī
Across = trāns (+ acc.)
Advance, I = prōgredior, prōgredī, prōgressus sum
Advise, I = moneō, -ēre, monuī, monitum
Affair = rēs, reī, f.
After (conjunction) = postquam; cum (+ pluperfect subjunctive)
After (preposition) = post (+ acc.)
Afterwards = posteā
Again = iterum
Against = contrā (+ acc.)
Alive = vīvus, -a, -um
All = omnis, -e
Allow, I = patior, patī, passus sum
Almost = paene
Alone = sōlus, -a, -um
Along = per (+ acc.)
Already – iam
Also = etiam; quoque
Although = quamquam; cum (+ imperfect subjunctive)
Always = semper
Am not willing, I = nōlō, nōlle, nōluī
Am willing, I = volō, velle, voluī
Am, I = sum, esse, fuī
Among = inter (+ acc.)
And = et; -que
And not = nec, neque
Anger = īra, -ae, f.
Angry = īrātus, -a, -um
Animal = animal, animālis, n.
Announce, I = nūntiō, -āre, -āvī, -ātum
Another = alius, alia, aliud
Answer, I = respondeō, -ēre, respondī, respōnsum
Approach, I = appropinquō, -āre, -āvī, -ātum (+ ad or + dative); adeō, adīre, adiī, aditum
Arms = arma, -ōrum, n. pl.
Army = exercitus, -ūs, m.
Around = circum (+ acc.)
Arrive, I = adveniō, -īre, advēnī, adventum
Arrow = sagitta, -ae, f.
Ask, I = rogō, -āre, -āvī, -ātum
At last = tandem
Attack, I = oppugnō, -āre, -āvī, -ātum

Bad = malus, -a, -um
Battle = proelium, -iī, n.
Bear, I = ferō, ferre, tulī, lātum (irreg.)
Beautiful = pulcher, pulchra, pulchrum
Because = quod
Because of = propter (+ acc.)
Before (conjunction) = antequam
Before (preposition) = ante (+ acc.)
Believe, I = crēdō, -ere, crēdidī, crēditum (+ dat.)
Between = inter (+ acc.)
Big = magnus, -a, -um
Body = corpus, corporis, n.
Bold = audāx, audācis
Book = liber, librī, m.
Both ... and = et ... et
Boy = puer, puerī, m.
Brave = fortis, -e
Bravely = fortiter
Bright = clārus, -a, -um
Brother = frāter, frātris, m.
Build, I = aedificō, -āre, -āvī, -ātum
But = sed
By chance = forte
Call, I = vocō, -āre, -āvī, -ātum
Capture, I = capiō, -ere, cēpī, captum
Carry, I = portō, -āre, -āvī, -ātum; ferō, ferre, tulī, lātum (irreg.)
Carry on, I = gerō, -ere, gessī, gestum
Catch sight of, I = cōnspiciō, -ere, cōnspexī, cōnspectum
Chance, by = forte
Chief = prīnceps, prīncipis, c.
Children = līberī, -ōrum, m. pl.
Choose, I = legō, legere, lēgī, lectum
Citizen = cīvis, cīvis, c.
City = urbs, urbis, f.
Clear = clārus, -a, -um
Collect, I = colligō, -ere, collēgī, collēctum
Come, I = veniō, venīre, vēnī, ventum
Come together, I = conveniō, -īre, convēnī, conventum
Companion = comes, comitis, c.; socius, -iī, m.
Compel, I = cōgō, cōgere, coēgī, coāctum
Concerning = dē (+ abl.)
Conquer, I = vincō, -ere, vīcī, victum
Country, fatherland = patria, -ae, f.

Courage = virtus, virtūtis, f.
Crowd = turba, -ae, f.
Cruel = crūdēlis, -e
Danger = perīculum, perīculī, n.
Daughter = fīlia, -ae, f. (dat. and abl. pl. = fīliābus)
Day = diēs, diēī, m. (fem. if an appointed day)
Dead = mortuus, -a, -um
Dear = cārus, -a, -um
Death = mors, mortis, f.
Decide, I = cōnstituō, -ere, cōnstituī, cōnstitūtum
Deep = altus, -a, -um
Defend, I = dēfendō, -ere, dēfendī, dēfēnsum
Delay = mōra, -ae, f.
Depart, I = discēdō, -ere, discessī, discessum
Destroy, I = dēleō, -ēre, dēlēvī, dēlētum
Die, I = pereō, -īre, -iī, -itum; morior, morī, mortuus sum
Difficult = difficilis, -e
Do not wish, I = nōlō, nōlle, nōluī
Do not ...! = nōlī/nōlīte (+ infin.)
Do, I = faciō, -ere, fēcī, factum
Down from = dē (+ abl.)
Drink, I = bibō, bibere, bibī
Drive, I = pellō, -ere, pepulī, pulsum
During: use ablative for time 'during which'
Easy = facilis, -e
Eat, I = cōnsūmō, -ere, cōnsūmpsī, cōnsūmptum
Eight = octo
Eighteen = duodēvīgintī
Eighth = octāvus, -a, -um
Eighty = octōgintā
Eleven = ūndecim
Encourage, I = hortor, -ārī, hortātus sum
Enemy = hostis, hostis, c. (usually used in plural)
Enter, I = intrō, -āre, -āvī, -ātum; ingredior, ingredī, ingressus sum
Escape, I = effugiō, -ere, effūgī
Even, also = etiam
Every = omnis, -e
Faith = fidēs, fideī, f.
Famous = clārus, -a, -um; nōtus, -a, -um
Farmer = agricola, -ae, m.
Father = pater, patris, m.
Fatherland = patria, -ae, f.
Fear, I = timeō, -ēre, timuī
Few = paucī, -ae, -a
Field = ager, agrī, m.
Fifteen = quīndecim
Fifth = quīntus, -a, -um
Fight, I = pugnō, -āre, -āvī, -ātum

Find, I = inveniō, -īre, invēnī, inventum
First = prīmus, -a, -um
Five = quīnque
Flee, I = fugiō, -ere, fūgī, fugitum
Follow, I = sequor, sequī, secutus sum
Food = cibus, cibī, m.
For = nam
For a long time = diū
Force, I = cōgō, cōgere, coēgī, coāctum
Forces = cōpiae, -ārum, f. pl.
Fortunate = fēlīx, fēlīcis
Forty = quadrāgintā
Four = quattuor
Fourteen = quattuordecim
Fourth = quārtus, -a, -um
Free, I = līberō, -āre, -āvī, -ātum
Friend = amīcus, amīcī, m.
Frighten, I = terreō, -ēre, terruī, territum
Frightened = perterritus, -a, -um
From = ā/ab (+ abl.)
Gift = dōnum, -ī, n.
Girl = puella, -ae, f.
Give, I = dō, dāre, dedī, dătum
Go, I = eō, īre, iī/īvī, itum
Go across, I = trānseō, -īre, -iī, -itum
Go back, I = redeō, -īre, -iī, -itum
Go in, I = ineō, inīre, iniī, initum; ingredior, ingredī, ingressus sum
Go out, I = exeō, exīre, exiī, exitum; ēgredior, ēgredī, ēgressus sum
God = deus, deī, m.
Goddess = dea, -ae, f. (dat. and abl. pl. = deābus)
Gold = aurum, -ī, n.
Good = bonus, -a, -um
Great = magnus, -a, -um
Greatly = magnopere
Greek = Graecus, -a, -um
Greet, I = salūtō, -āre, -āvī, -ātum
Ground = terra, -ae, f.
Guard = custōs, custōdis, m.
Guard, I = custōdiō, -īre, -īvī, -ītum
Hand = manus, -ūs, f.
Hand over, I = trādō, -ere, trādidī, trāditum
Happy = laetus, -a, -um
Harbour = portus, -ūs, m.
Have, I = habeō, -ēre, habuī, habitum
Hear, I = audiō, audīre, audīvī, audītum
Help = auxilium, -iī, n.
Help, I = iuvō, iuvāre, iūvī, iūtum

Her (own) = suus, -a, -um
Here = hīc
Herself (reflexive) = sē
High = altus, -a, -um
Himself (reflexive) = sē
His (own) = suus, -a, -um
Hold, I = teneō, -ēre, tenuī, tentum
Hope = spēs, speī, f.
Horse = equus, equī, m.
Hour = hōra, -ae, f.
House = domus, -ūs, f.
How = quam
However = autem; tamen (neither should be written
    as the 1st word in a clause)
Huge = ingēns, ingentis
Hurry, I = festīnō, -āre, -āvī, -ātum; contendō,
    contendere, contendī, contentum
Husband = coniūnx, coniugis, m.
I = egŏ
Immediately = statim
In = in (+ abl.)
In front of = prō (+ abl.)
In order to = ut (+ subjunctive)
In vain = frūstrā
Inhabitant = incola, -ae, c.
Into = in (+ acc.)
Island = īnsula, -ae, f.
Its (own) = suus, -a, -um
Itself (reflexive) = sē
Journey = iter, itineris, n.
Kill, I = necō, -āre, -āvī, -ātum; occīdō, -ere, occīdī,
    occīsum; interficiō, -ere, interfēcī, interfectum
King = rēx, rēgis, m.
Land = terra, -ae, f.
Laugh, I = rīdeō, -ēre, rīsī, rīsum
Lead, I = dūcō, dūcere, dūxī, ductum
Lead back, I = redūcō, -ere, redūxī, reductum
Leader = dux, ducis, m.; prīnceps, prīncipis, c.
Leave, I = relinquō, -ere, relīquī, relictum
Lest, in order that … not = ne (+ subjunctive)
Light = lūx, lūcis, f.
Like, I = amō, -āre, -āvī, -ātum
Listen (to), I = audiō, audīre, audīvī, audītum
Little = parvus, -a, -um
Live (in), I = habitō, -āre, -āvī, -ātum
Long = longus, -a, -um
Lord = dominus, dominī, m.
Love, I = amō, -āre, -āvī, -ātum
Make, I = faciō, -ere, fēcī, factum
Make for, I = petō, -ere, petīvī, petītum

Man (as opposed to woman) = vir, virī, m.
Man (human) = homō, hominis, c.
Many = multus, -a, -um
March, I = contendō, contendere, contendī,
    contentum
Master, lord = dominus, dominī, m.
Master, teacher = magister, magistrī, m.
Meanwhile = intereā
Meet, I = conveniō, -īre, convēnī, conventum
Messenger = nūntius, nūntiī, m.
Middle = medius, -a, -um
Miserable = miser, misera, miserum
Missile = tēlum, -ī, n.
Moreover = autem (not written as the 1st word in a clause)
Mother = māter, mātris, f.
Mountain = mōns, montis, m.
Move, I = moveō, -ēre, mōvī, mōtum
Much = multus, -a, -um
Name = nōmen, nōminis, n.
Near = prope (+ acc.)
Never = numquam
New = novus, -a, -um
Night = nox, noctis, f.
Nine = novem
Nineteen = ūndēvīgintī
Ninety = nōnāgintā
Ninth = nōnus, -a, -um
No one = nēmō, nūllius, c.
Noble = nōbilis, -e
Nor = nec, neque
Not = nōn
Nothing = nihil
Now = iam; nunc
Often = saepe
Old man = senex, senis, m.
On = in (+ abl.)
On account of = propter (+ acc.)
On behalf of = prō (+ abl.)
On to = in (+ acc.)
Once upon a time = ōlim
One = ūnus
One hundred = centum
One thousand = mīlle
Or = aut
Order, I = iubeō, -ēre, iussī, iussum; impero, -āre,
    -āvī, -ātum (+ dat.)
Other = alius, alia, aliud
Others = cēterī, -ae, -a
Ought, I = dēbeō, -ēre, dēbuī, dēbitum
Our = noster, nostra, nostrum

Out of = ē/ex (+ abl.)

Over = super (+ acc.)

Overcome, I = superō, -āre, -āvī, -ātum

Owe, I = dēbeō, -ēre, dēbuī, dēbitum

Parent = parēns, parentis, c.

Part = pars, partis, f.

People = gēns, gentis, f.

Perish, I = pereō, -īre, -iī, -itum

Persuade, I = persuādeō, -ēre, persuāsī, persuāsum (+ dat.)

Place = locus, -ī, m.

Place, I = pōnō, -ere, posuī, positum

Play, I = lūdō, -ere, lūsī, lūsum

Poet = poēta, -ae, m.

Praise, I = laudō, -āre, -āvī, -ātum

Prepare, I = parō, -āre, -āvī, -ātum

Present, I am = adsum, adesse, adfuī

Promise = fidēs, fideī, f.

Proud = superbus, -a, -um

Punish, I = pūniō, -īre, pūnīvī, pūnītum

Queen = rēgīna, -ae, f.

Quick = celer, celeris, celere

Quickly = celeriter

Race = gēns, gentis, f.

Read, I = legō, legere, lēgī, lectum

Receive, I = accipiō, -ere, accēpī, acceptum

Relate, I = nārrō, -āre, -āvī, -ātum

Remain, I = maneō, -ēre, mānsī, mānsum

Report, I = nūntiō, -āre, -āvī, -ātum

Rest, the = cēterī, -ae, -a

Return, I: see Go back

Reward = praemium, -iī, n.

River = flūmen, flūminis, n.

Road = via, -ae, f.

Roman = Rōmānus, -a, -um

Rule, I = regō, regere, rēxī, rēctum

Run, I = currō, currere, cucurrī, cursum

Rush, I = ruō, -ere, ruī, rutum

Sacred = sacer, sacra, sacrum

Sad = trīstis, -e

Safe = tūtus, -a, -um

Sail, I = nāvigō, -āre, -āvī, -ātum

Sailor = nauta, -ae, m.

Same = īdem, eadem, idem

Savage = saevus, -a, -um

Save, I = servō, -āre, -āvī, -ātum

Say, I = dīcō, dīcere, dīxī, dictum

Say, they (quoting direct speech) = inquiunt

Says, he/she (quoting direct speech) = inquit

Schoolmaster = magister, magistrī, m.

Sea = mare, maris, n.

Second = secundus, -a, -um

See, I = videō, -ēre, vīdī, vīsum

Seek, I = petō, -ere, petīvī, petītum

Seize (a place), I = occupō, -āre, -āvī, -ātum

Self = ipse, ipsa, ipsum

Send, I = mittō, mittere, mīsī, missum

Set out, I = proficīscor, proficīscī, profectus sum

Seven = septem

Seventeen = septendecim

Seventh = septimus, -a, -um

Seventy = septuāgintā

Shield = scūtum, scūtī, n.

Ship = nāvis, nāvis, f.

Shout = clāmor, clāmōris, m.

Shout, I = clāmō, -āre, -āvī, -ātum

Show, I = ostendō, -ere, ostendī, ostentum

Since = cum (+ imperfect subjunctive)

Sing, I = cantō, -āre, -āvī, -ātum

Sister = soror, sorōris, f.

Six = sex

Sixteen = sēdecim

Sixth = sextus, -a, -um

Sixty = sexāgintā

Sky = caelum, -ī, n.

Slave = servus, servī, m.

Slave-girl = ancilla, -ae, f.

Sleep = somnus, -ī, m.

Sleep, I = dormiō, -īre, -īvī, -ītum

Slowly = lentē

Small = parvus, -a, -um

So, thus = sīc

Soldier = mīles, mīlitis, m.

Son = fīlius, fīliī, m.

Soon = mox

Speak, I = loquor, loquī, locūtus sum

Spear = hasta, -ae, f.; tēlum, -ī, n.

Stand, I = stō, -āre, stetī, stătum

Storm = tempestās, -ātis, f.

Street = via, -ae, f.

Strive, I = contendō, contendere, contendī, contentum

Strong = fortis, -e; validus, -a, -um

Suddenly = subitō

Suffer, I = patior, patī, passus sum

Surely ... = nōnne? (introduces a question expecting the answer 'yes')

Surely ... not = num? (introduces a question expecting the answer 'no')

Swift = celer, celeris, celere

Sword = gladius, gladiī, m.
Take, I = capiō, -ere, cēpī, captum
Task = labor, labōris, m.
Tell, I = nārrō, -āre, -āvī, -ātum
Temple = templum, templī, n.
Ten = decem
Tenth = decimus, -a, -um
Terrified = perterritus, -a, -um
Terrify, I = terreō, -ēre, terruī, territum
That (near me) = is, ea, id
That (over there) = ille, illa, illud
Their (own) = suus, -a, -um
Themselves (reflexive) = sē
Then = deinde; tum
There = ibi
Therefore = igitur; itaque
Thing = rēs, reī, f.
Third = tertius, -a, -um
Thirteen = tredecim
Thirty = trīgintā
This = hic, haec, hoc
Three = trēs
Through = per (+ acc.)
Throw, I = iaciō, -ere, iēcī, iactum
Thus = sīc
Tired = fessus, -a, -um
To (towards) = ad (+ acc.)
Tomorrow = crās
Towards = ad (+ acc.)
Town = oppidum, oppidī, n.
Trust = fidēs, fideī, f.
Trust, I = crēdō, -ere, crēdidī, crēditum (+ dat.)
Try, I = conor, -ārī, conātus sum
Twelve = duodecim
Twenty = vīgintī
Two = duǒ
Under = sub (+ abl.)
Unhappy = miser, misera, miserum
Urge, I = hortor, -ārī, hortātus sum
Voice = vōx, vōcis, f.
Wait for, I = exspectō, -āre, -āvī, -ātum
Wall = mūrus, mūrī, m.
Wander, I = errō, -āre, -āvī, -ātum

Want, I = cupiō, -ere, cupīvī, cupītum
War = bellum, bellī, n.
Warn, I = moneō, -ēre, monuī, monitum
Watch, I = spectō, -āre, -āvī, -ātum
Water = aqua, -ae, f.
Wave = unda, -ae, f.
We = nōs
Weapons = arma, -ōrum, n. pl.
Wear, I = gerō, -ere, gessī, gestum
Weather = tempestās, -ātis, f.
Well = bene
Well-known = nōtus, -a, -um
What? = quid?
When = ubi; cum (+ pluperfect subjunctive)
Where? = ubi?
While = dum; cum (+ imperfect subjunctive);
Who? = quis?
Whole = tōtus, -a, -um (goes like ūnus)
Why? = cūr?
Wife = coniūnx, coniugis, f.; uxor, uxōris, f.
Wind = ventus, -ī, m.
Wine = vīnum, -ī, n.
Wise = sapiēns, sapientis
Wish, I = volō, velle, voluī
With (together with) = cum (+ abl.)
Within (of time): use ablative of time 'within which'
Without = sine (+ abl.)
Woman = fēmina, -ae, f.; mulier, mulieris, f.
Word = verbum, verbī, n.
Work = labor, labōris, m.; opus, operis, n.
Work, I = labōrō, -āre, -āvī, -ātum
Wound = vulnus, vulneris, n.
Wound, I = vulnerō, -āre, -āvī, -ātum
Wretched = miser, misera, miserum
Write, I = scrībō, -ere, scrīpsī, scriptum
Year = annus, -ī, m.
Yesterday = herī
You (pl.) = vōs
You (sing.) = tū
Young man = iuvenis, iuvenis, m.
Your (of you (pl.)) = vester, vestra, vestrum
Your (of you (sing.)) = tuus, -a, -um

Index

Index